Just in time!

Just in time!

Derek C. James

Inter-Varsity Press

INTER-VARSITY PRESS
Universities and Colleges Christian Fellowship
38 De Montfort Street, Leicester LE1 7GP

© INTER-VARSITY PRESS, LEICESTER, ENGLAND

First edition 1977

ISBN 0 85110 455 X

Illustrations by Leon Baxter

Printed in Great Britain by
C. Nicholls & Company Ltd
The Philips Park Press, Manchester

Contents

Preface	7
1 Here beginneth...	11
2 God is dead	20
3 ...but he won't lie down!	31
4 Jesus is God	44
5 The proof of the pudding...	54
6 ...is in the eating	67
7 A bed of roses?	80
8 Happy families!	93
9 All one body we!	103
10 The end is nigh!	113

Preface

Should you chance to have opened this book as far as the Preface, I feel that a word of explanation would be in keeping with regard to the title. I think more time was spent on formulating these three words than on the whole of the book put together. A number of generous friends assisted me with the problem of a title by making all kinds of helpful suggestions, such as *How to find out all you need to know what a good many other people discovered a long time ago*. Now this struck me as being a trifle too long, so another friend suggested *Just right*. But somehow, neither title seemed to fit in with my theme. However, in desperation, it did in fact occur to me as I lay on my pillow in the night watches (beds are hard to come by these days), that if I didn't think of a title soon then the whole project would be in jeopardy. Thus, whilst in a suitably soporific frame of mind, the idea became apparent – just in time, so to speak!

This doesn't tell you much about the title, I suppose, and really, for you to get its subtle significance, I would have to write a book on the subject – which point would seem to lead us naturally into chapter one. However, just before I do so, I feel I must tell you that the book is overtly pro-Christian, and if you reckon that at this stage you cannot stomach such reading material, then for you it may be too late already. On the other hand I am of the opinion that most people, at some stage in their lives, reach a point when they realize, either through bitter experience or through sensible reasoning, that life is not all booze, birds and bands. They come to see that there must be some purpose in life beyond the acquisition of things or position, and that, in some vague way, this purpose is linked with a divine Being.

If this is your position, then you have reached it just in time. For, provided you can tolerate my ridiculously practical attitude and outlook, coupled with the occasional euphonium (or is it euphemism?), then indeed you may find this book of some help. Its contents are based upon twenty years of practical experience in dealing with genuine difficulties with which many young people have grappled concerning the Christian faith. It is not aimed specifically at youth, but more at the people, be they young or old, middle-aged or of uncertain vintage, who want to consider the basics of Christianity without all the trappings of conventional traditionalism that dog every branch of the faith from extreme Catholicism to the most miraculous Evangelical. The author does not believe that one has to go through a predetermined formula before being able to meet with Jesus Christ in all his fullness, whether that formula is a series of rites, such as Baptism, Confirmation or Communion, or a series of doctrines and experiences, valuable though all of these things might be. On the contrary, I believe you can meet with Christ in whatever circumstances you might be placed, and that such a meeting can be real, vital, continuous and ordinary. What is more, I am convinced that many professing Christians have missed much, if not all, of the relevance of their faith. I have never been a visionary in the literal sense of the word, but I am of the opinion that a good number of my fellow believers are totally inept at recognizing the Christ of their everyday experience. They claim the presence of God with one breath and deny him with the next, in that they seem unable to recognize a continued meeting with or 'vision' of Christ in all their daily experiences.

The basic cause of this is a failure to understand what God has done and is doing on our behalf, and I hope that this book will help the uncommitted (and many who think they are committed) to recognize Christ as one who can be and is with them all the time, and that in such a recognition they will come to experience the real and genuine happiness (as opposed to much modern-day effervescence) that comes from a life committed to him in all its detail.

DEREK C. JAMES
Southampton, 1976

1 Here beginneth...

Did you know that nowadays only thirty per cent of the population believe in hell? You didn't? Well, there you are, you see. And here's another useless piece of information for you – the seal population in the Wash has doubled over the last five years. Of course, for most of us, hell is associated only with banner-waving fanatics and old-fashioned sandwich-men who can still be seen on occasions in the great metropolis. Trapped between their boards they seem totally unaware of the realities of life before them or the scorn they attract behind them. Should we ever chance to darken the doors of a church (and for many that is obviously a most unlikely prospect), we would be amazed if we even heard the word 'hell' mentioned at all. But then, who wants to go to church these days anyway? In most of our minds the church is only one stage removed from the sandwich-men.

We shall be returning to the first theme at a later stage in the book; but thinking of church for a moment – you know a lot of funny things happen there. On one occasion my friend and I went to a campaign meeting which was being conducted by a particularly fervent evangelist. From time to time the meeting was disturbed by equally fervent believers who persisted in calling out 'Praise the Lord!' to every other phrase the preacher uttered. As this good gentleman was staying with us at the time I knew that he found this rather distracting; but on this particular evening he caught them.

'Everybody knows', he said, 'that the most famous man this age has ever known...'

'Praise the Lord!' came the usual interruptions.

'... the man who has done more than anyone else for this generation...'

'Praise his name!' continued the opposition.

'... the man to whom we owe the greatest debt of all...'

'Hallelujah! Yes! Yes!' By now they had reached a fervent crescendo.

'... is Winston Churchill!' concluded the preacher.

My friend and I, not to mention other perverse characters in the congregation, found great difficulty in self-restraint, while those of a more sober frame of mind turned various colours, all of which may be found in our glorious national flag. Of course they were expecting the name to be Jesus Christ. The preacher was perhaps a little unkind, but it had the desired effect!

Apart from these occasional interludes which do tend to relieve the monotony, church, I must confess, is frequently a poor advertisement for the faith. I shall have more to say about this in a later chapter, but by way of introduction let me say how tragic it is that increasingly the Christian faith is judged by the popular press and the mass media in terms of church services. Daily, weekly, both local and national radio churn out the set liturgy for the day, or the usual 'hymn-prayer-hymn' sandwich (if it happens to be the turn of the Nonconformists), and Mr Average, who may chance to tune in, comes to the conclusion with some justification that the church has nothing to offer him. In any case, as he cannot understand what it is saying even when he does happen to listen, he concludes inevitably that its message is meaningless.

Sometimes our mythical man may pass through the portals and venture inside the sacred building. It is cold and uninviting. The notice-board is littered with scraps of paper fraying at the edges, conveying bits of information as useless as that produced by Neville Chamberlain just prior to the Second World War. The books are musty and the Bible Authorized; the seats are hard and the heaters high – not to mention the theology; the statues are made of marble and the people are made of stone.

Of course, some will say, our church is not like that. We make everybody feel welcome. 'Come and join us, brother', we say, with an enthusiasm not unlike that of an angler catching an unwary fish. Soon we get down to some good hearty singing to warm us up, which is more than the gas-fired heaters are likely to do; they seem to have lost all their enthusiasm for high-speed gas these days. 'When the roll is rocked up yonder, I'll be there,' we all start to sing – at least, that's what it sounds like.

Then there are the people. They are so terribly middle class. In some cases they try their best to make you feel welcome, but it all seems rather unreal. There is a barrier. Yet it is not the kind of barrier of which they are aware. They assume that, because they are Christians and Mr Average is not, then that makes for a barrier. But this is not the case. Jesus never felt such barriers between him and those whom he met day by day. In fact, the only people who seemed to be a real barrier to him were the religious leaders! Perhaps there is a message here somewhere. Mr Average is not quite sure where the barrier lies, but he knows that when he is in church it is like being a fish out of water. If it is God's house then he would rather stay outside, because God is cold and has a different cultural background from him. God, he reckons, reads *The Daily Telegraph*, whereas he reads *The Sun*; God prefers Grammar Schools whereas he went to a Secondary Modern School; God says 'blast' whereas he says 'bloody'; God drinks Sauterne whereas he drinks Tankard – and who wants God under these terms?

Sometimes Mr Average has actually met a real live Christian. He seems a little bit 'other-worldly', though he tends to dress the same. Mr Average has knocked up against him at work. In fact, he first noticed him in the canteen. He had been around the building for some time and he seemed like all the other fellows; but when he sat down to his meal he had a strange habit of bowing his head for a brief second. Mr Average thought at first that he was inspecting his tie; he certainly looked at it very intently as if he had lost a gold clip or the like.

'Say, George. Why do you look at yer tie every time you start a meal?'

George looked pained.

'I am thanking the Lord for my food,' he said diffidently.

'Cor lumme. Who on earth would want to thank the Lord for this rubbish?'

The conversation continued at this rather low level

'Thank the Lord for this rubbish?'

for some time, a thing which caused George to question in his mind whether or not he was truly witnessing for the Lord. But then Mr Average started to question him about his belief in God.

'How do you know there's a God, then? Have you ever seen him?'

'Well, no,' faltered George.

'Has he ever spoken to you?'

'Oh, yes ... er ... well, not exactly.'

'What do you mean – "Not exactly"?'

'Well, I haven't actually heard a voice,' continued George. 'Yet I know that he is there. I feel it, you see, for it says in the Word, "I will never leave thee, nor forsake thee", and I cling to this promise and I'm sure that God is with me all the time, every day. Yes! Every moment of every day...'

Maybe George was right, but Mr Average was no longer with him. He did not wish to remain with him any moment of any day, more than was absolutely necessary. George seemed so out of contact with the real world. He had standards which he thought were so vital, yet when it came to real life situations where real values were being fought out – George was nowhere to be seen. He was never at the Union meeting, maybe because he was always praying somewhere. He seemed so busy about his Christian life that he had no time for the inequalities of the factory floor or the educational system. George seemed to expect him to leave all these things behind in favour of his Middle-Class God, but Mr Average was not interested. In any case no person with any sense believed the Bible these days, for Science had proved it to be wrong, and when it came to loving your neighbour, Mr Average had seen more

Christianity in the pub than he had in churches. Mind you, he had been in more pubs than churches, but that was totally irrelevant. In fact, come to think of it, he could not remember the last time he went to church. Which thought seems to bring us back to our first paragraph.

Perhaps this digressive caricature of two people's views of the Christian faith may ring a bell with you. There is a feeling inside you which says you would like to know more about God, even if only to dismiss him from your mind. In fact you try to do just that, but somehow or other the thought of God seems to rear its ugly head on a number of unsuspecting occasions. You have tackled some of the believers about their faith, but their answers are either contradictory or unsatisfactory. Meanwhile you occupy yourself in your legitimate business, and in other business whose legitimacy is doubtful, and it is on these occasions that you get a nasty feeling about God. But where to turn? The church seems hopelessly inadequate.

Maybe, on the other hand, you are like George, who does not really feel that he is getting anywhere with his Christian faith. Maybe, just maybe, he has not got any *real* faith. Perish the thought! But yet, why is it that with monotonous regularity one meets so many who have professed 'conversion' yet never made the grade? It would seem that the modern fall-out rate puts an atomic explosion into a total eclipse. Some might say that the seed has 'fallen on stony ground' and to a certain extent that could be true. But in the case of many others they have been presented with a false, culture-biased and often class-ridden standard of what is required in order to grow as a Christian. As a result they have been genuinely put off.

Well, whatever your position, I think the next few chapters could help you. They are overtly Christian, but not the kind of Christianity you are thinking about. They are uncompromisingly religious, but not the sort of religion that is churned out on the telly each week. They are aimed at bringing you into a real experience of Christ, but not at the expense of your mind, emotions or will. I ask only one condition of you as you read these pages, a condition sadly lacking from much that goes by the name of Christianity today. Furthermore, it is blatantly absent from many other fields of life, notably those of politics and big business. The one condition to which I refer is that of *honesty*. If you are going to get anything of real value out of this book, then you must be perfectly honest with yourself. Now this is not easy. Some have gone so far with their self-deception that they are deluded into a false way of life, and this to such an extent that no-one seems able to help them. Let me illustrate.

If you saw a blind man walking to the edge of a cliff, what would you do? Phone for the TV cameras? What a story it would make! You can see the headline captions now: 'Mystery man walks to his death. Our man on the spot was there to record the last fleeting moments of blind Mr X who plunged 900 feet to his death this morning. . . .'

Or would you, perhaps, look the other way? 'Pass by on the other side' is the phrase, I believe. No, of course not. At risk to your own life, you would run to try and stop him. You would shout at the top of your voice and warn him that he was approaching a 900-foot drop (or 274 metres, for those who must think metrically). Given the opportunity, you would physically restrain him from continuing along his suicidal path. But then when he struggles free, so he thinks, and walks over the edge with deliberate step, you can only stand with your mouth drooping in amazement. You did your best! What more could you have done? Did he not know he was near a cliff? Of course he did; you told him! It seemed as if he wanted to take the plunge. You warned him; but he did not face up to the truth because he just could not see it for himself. He did not really believe you; that was the trouble.

People today are blind! They are deluding themselves into thinking that all is well with their lives. But all is not well. Even the most amoral individual must be aware of that, however faintly. So if you want to stand a chance of seeing anything in these next few chapters, then you will need to open your eyes just a little. Not too much, for the light is dazzling. But the first step towards this 'revelation' is honesty. Take this step and maybe you will see something you have never seen before.

2 God is dead

I can think of no better place to begin than at the beginning. Another book, somewhat better known than mine, also had the same idea, for it started with the thought, 'In the beginning God ...'! In fact, this suggests to us the first real stumbling-block to the Christian faith, for the Bible never at any time seeks to prove the existence of God. It starts straight away with the assumption that God is there. Indeed, it goes as far as to say that anybody who thinks otherwise is a fool. Now that is not a very complimentary thing to say to a prospective convert, so in order not to cause you any embarrassment, I will refrain from saying it. (It's true though!) But we're still left asking, 'How do we know that God exists?'

It is the current outlook in many circles to explain away God as a figment of one's imagination, a necessary projection of man's inner self which serves to satisfy the weak but is of no value whatsoever to the strong-thinking man of today. Now you would expect such thoughts to find their way into a basically atheistic society, as indeed they do. But it is also true to say that some notable church dignitaries have been explaining away God as a rather embarrassing extra which the Christian church could well do without. You know the kind of thing – God is what you make of him; heaven is where you are, and all that sort of rot.

Heaven is where you are...

How naïve can you get? Imagine, my circumstances at work being heaven! It is enough to drive anybody to atheism.

When they find themselves on a sticky wicket, an interesting trick of politicians and churchmen is to do one of two things: either they shout loudly at their opponent, pouring ridicule on his views in the hope that if they make enough noise he will go away, or they show complete indifference to the problem in hand, pretending it does not exist. In quite a number of cases this is also true of those who do not believe in God.

An example of the first approach is to be found in a pamphlet produced by the British Humanist Association entitled *Moral Education in Secondary Schools*. The basic premise of the humanist is that of atheism and in a five-year course of Social Studies they relegate 'Religions' to one term's work in the fourth year. It is recommended that these 'Religions' are studied under the following headings: 'Primitive ignorance and fear. Need for security, dreams of immortality. Examples of good and harm caused by religion. Infancy and adolescence of mankind; Humanism; science; learning to live with reality.' The only book recommended for further reading is *The Humanist Revolution*. God is conspicuous by his absence and Christ is not even in for a mention. God is not there, anyway, for the subject-matter makes it clear that religion is based on ignorance and fear and that reality is to be found only in humanism and science. This kind of indoctrination is based on the unproved assumption that God is dead. If you assume that he is, and shout loud enough out of all proportion to your numbers or the logic of your argument, he will go away, perhaps. The trouble is, God is taking a long time to get the message! Someone will have to tell him!

Incidentally, it should be noted that this pamphlet was published in 1967 and is quoted merely as an example of the point being raised, not for the value of the arguments being expressed. As its approach has had little effect on Religious Education in schools, the British Humanist Association has recently pursued a different line of attack, appearing more as an angel of light suitably disguised in a booklet entitled *Objective, Fair and Balanced*. I mention this simply to indicate that the humanist has subsequently shifted his ground, at the same time pointing out that the significance of the quotation from the original pamphlet still remains for the purposes of my argument.

The second approach is more subtle and much more difficult to deal with. The likelihood is that you, the reader, belong to this second group. God may be there, and some certainly like to think so. What is more, if people want to worship him, then you would fight to the death to defend their right to do so. For you, however, he has no significance at all and you will choose to ignore him, not because you are unable to believe in him but because for you the word 'God' has no meaning. And yet the question keeps bothering you: 'Can we know for certain God is *not* there?' Surely he *is* dead as far as this generation is concerned?

Many years ago a young student philosopher by the name of Nietzsche rebelled in more senses than one against the Christian faith, particularly when it came to questions of morality. One night he was reported to have painted on the university's main wall in large letters,

'God is dead – Nietzsche'.

Next day the university was buzzing with amused comment. But by the following day the wording had been changed. Now it read,

'Nietzsche is dead – God'!

Just another student prank? Probably. Or more likely some rather over-enthusiastic Christians belonging to the church militant. Nonetheless, when his time came, Nietzsche died of tertiary syphilis, a disease he contracted as a student which led to insanity before his eventual death.

Now I am not suggesting that there is any connection between the writing on the wall and Nietzsche's death. But his total rejection of God led him to reject for the most part the Christian faith and its related moral standards. It was this latter rejection that eventually led to his death, for the fact remains that if God is dead there is really nothing to live for. Let us eat, drink and be merry, for tomorrow we die. And this is, of course, the chief object in life for many. Furthermore, if God is dead, then so are we all; life ends at the grave.

But many would say that he is not dead. Yet how do they know? Few claim to have seen God, and those who do make such claims are usually dismissed as cranks. How can you believe in a God whom you have never seen? The Bible itself says that 'No man has seen God at any time', so how can his existence be proved to a generation that starts out from a basis of complete scepticism?

Well, first of all, let us look at this word 'prove'. It is an unfortunate word when used in a religious context, for it implies that if we are unable to 'prove' that God is real in the mathematical sense of the word, then it automatically follows that he is not real. Yet in many other walks of life such proof of a similar nature is neither required nor even asked for.

Take music, for example. I think most people have heard of Handel, even if he does not turn you on – if you get my meaning! He wrote some jazz called 'Water Music' which you may or may not appreciate. Now in order to enjoy the delights of Handel it is not necessary for you to prove that the long-haired gentleman was real. The music itself is sufficient 'proof' that someone wrote the piece at a particular point in time. Call him Handel or Fred – it doesn't really matter. As it happens there is plenty of 'proof' that he existed and that he wrote the 'Water Music', but this is not the point. You do not need such proof to appreciate his work.

Now the same is true of God. No-one will be able to 'prove' to you in the mathematical sense of the word that God is there. But this does not in any sense lessen the likelihood of his existence or stop you from appreciating his presence. You may prefer God to appear to you in person. But I can assure you that he has no intention of making such a revelation – to you, or to anybody else for that matter. You may even say with another well-known character, 'Unless I see . . ., I will not believe.' But this will not impress God sufficiently for him to change the way he works. For, just as the reality of Handel's existence is expressed through the ever-present fact and reality of his music, so the reality of God's presence is expressed through the ever-present fact of his Spirit, whose music can be heard all around by those who care to listen and whose handiwork can be seen and experienced in a variety of different ways by those who care to look.

Now there are many realms into which you could peep if you want to get a glimpse of this God but, as I warned you on page 19, too bright a vision would be bad for your eyesight. I will limit myself, therefore, to only one aspect in this chapter, and to two more in the succeeding chapters. They are views which are developed in full and the first concerns the world about us.

One of the perennial queries about God is evoked by the so-called opposition between the Bible and science. The argument is often voiced with little previous thought and usually goes something like this: 'Christians say that God made heaven and earth in six days, but scientists say that it all evolved. They cannot both be right and I would prefer to put my shirt on evolution.' Now I do not wish to get bogged down in this kind of discussion, but just a few pertinent remarks may be made before I move on. If you read Genesis chapter one carefully you will discover that it does not say that God made heaven and earth in six days. In fact it says that 'In the beginning God created the heavens and the earth . . .' and the phrase 'In the beginning' can cover as many millions of years as you care to mention, or only a few seconds. Genesis chapter one is basically a re-formation story, not a creation story. The word 'create' occurs only three times, in verses 1, 21 and 27; in all the other examples various aspects of creation are 'made' to appear, such as in verse 7. Here a Hebrew word is used different from that meaning 'create'. In other words we can argue, if we wish, that the means for its development were already built into the original creation; just the right environment was the thing that was lacking.

It is this word 'made' or 'constituted', rather than the word 'create', which is used in those passages in the Old Testament where it says that God made heaven and earth in six days, such as in Exodus 20:11. Furthermore, the word 'day' could well be translated as 'age', or 'period of time', rather than a literal twenty-four hours, and there are many who believe that this is its meaning in Genesis 1. Be that as it may, the point I am making is that it is not particularly vital what view you hold about *how* man and his world were made, for it makes no difference to the existence of God or to the all-important point that God created everything. It is this supreme principle that the writer of Genesis is expressing. As to *how* God created it all, he neither knew nor cared.

Now I consider that this is not only true, but decidedly logical. And this is the 'burden' of this chapter, to use a medieval word. As I write I am surrounded by a great variety of objects of varying beauty. On the window-sill is a picture of my wife – enough said! Words fail me! On my desk is a typewriter; to my left a metal tray made of twisted wire; farther over, a duplicator, and so on. Now let us take the desk. It is of simple design, the maker had the user in view and it was given to me by my wife as a wedding present. At one time the wood was growing on a tree. (Brace yourselves, there are more startling revelations to come!) Now the wood did not say to itself,

'I'm getting bored with being stuck up this tree all day. I know what I'll do. I'll come down from this tree and make myself into a desk.'

No, of course not! The tree had to be felled, sawn and distributed to the cabinet-maker. The desk had to be be planned with exact measurements so that the carpenter could cut the logs to the right size. They had to be fashioned, shaped, glued and screwed! The finished article then needed to be polished, packed and delivered. Just imagine the amount of thinking and planning that went into the production of my desk. Yet look at the result – oh, sorry, you can't see it. Well, it's functional, but I wouldn't exactly describe it as a Chippendale. Now the same could be said a hundred times for all the articles that surround me in my room. Each one represents the mental efforts of many human beings, probably running into hundreds, if not thousands.

Yet, as I look further afield out of my window, I am enabled to look over a panoramic view of Southampton Sports Centre – in the summer, that is. In the winter the workmen block out part of the view with some revolting man-made objects called sight-screens, but that is another story. My eye settles on lines of trees, each of varying shapes and sizes; stretches of grass support the antics of children at their games, while spotted dogs scurry about the cricket pitches leaving the inevitable record of their presence. Squirrels leap from bough to bough; robins peck the worms from the patch of ground I dug yesterday, while the stream at the bottom of the garden bubbles busily down to the Test. (Idyllic, is it not?) Did all these things just happen by chance? Did the squirrel say to itself, 'I want to be a squirrel'?

Did the oak tree develop its own frame independent of all other creation? And what human being can make grass – that commodity which all of us rot down for compost each year, yet it possesses in its texture a system of veins which knocks my cumbersome old desk into a cocked hat.

If all the clumsy and often unattractive objects that surround me in my room had to be planned and made, how much more the other objects which I see outside my immediate environment! It requires much more faith on my part to believe that they came as a result of chance than to believe that they were made by an all-wise God. Whether or not the method God used was evolution is not important. The fact is that these things of beauty which surround us are a living witness to the one who made them, just as Handel's music is 'proof' that someone of genius, call him Handel or any other name, composed music which has stood the test of time.

This is called the argument from design, as I am sure many of you will realize. No doubt you will also know that frequently efforts have been made to show that it does not prove the existence of God. I am not, however, setting out to 'prove' that God is there, but merely to demonstrate his presence. My sole purpose is to put the question to you, 'Which is easier, to believe that it all happened by chance (for such a view is quite definitely an act of faith, make no mistake about it) or to believe that it was made by God?' You may prefer to call this person by a name other than God, such as 'Divine Influence'. All right. It is of little importance what name you give him, but it is preferable if we all give him the same name for the sake of continuity. So for the purposes of this book he shall be called 'God'. Meanwhile, if I come across any better answer to the question, 'Who made the world?' I will let you know. For the time being – my money is on God!

3 ... but he won't lie down!

We live in the day of Opinion Polls and are constantly bombarded with their 'assured results'. Some Christians see such polls as 'the work of the devil', apparently because they predict the future. My only thought on the matter is that I never have had a great deal of confidence in the devil. Nonetheless, it is generally accepted that if you take a number of polls and lump together their findings, then you do get a fairly reasonable indication of people's views. This is the case with regard to belief in God. The vast majority believe in some sort of divine being although, admittedly, their assessment of this superior power or divine influence tends to vary as frequently as the number of people who express views on the subject.

Because of this, however, I am of the opinion that the questions about God which are in the minds of most people these days are not so much concerned with his existence, but more with what he is like. How would we recognize him? Why does he allow so much suffering? Who made God in the first place? Surely all religions point to the same God? These are typical examples of the queries in the minds of many people and I am not the first to attempt to answer some of them. Of course there are a number of folk whose view of the 'divine influence' is rather limited. J. B. Phillips had just this point in mind when he wrote his book, *Your God is too Small*. In the first part he lists a number of the popular views of God, all of which cut him down to size and paint a portrait of a God that is decidedly man-shaped. God is like a policeman, ready to crack down upon us when we break the law, or he is a Grand Old Man rather like Father Christmas, distributing largesse, not to mention presents, to all he meets. Then there are those who tend to look upon God as a permanent fire-alarm – always there in the case of an emergency but deliberately ignored when all is going well.

Now if in all honesty you do think there is a 'divine influence' somewhere around, then you are in a good position to discover more about him, for the Lord tends to help those who are searching for him. If you draw near to God there is every certainty that he will draw near to you. So, before we tackle the second of our three points mentioned on page 26, let us take a look at some of these questions about God's existence which genuinely afflict the minds of those who want to get to know more about him. Then, perhaps, we shall be able to see more clearly when we move on in later chapters to a more personal view of God.

Since I put forward a case for the existence of God in the previous chapter, it would seem appropriate to commence with the perennial plum, 'Who made God?' The question is a very human one and for this reason alone it is difficult for the answer to be fully understood. In some respects the answer is quite simple, but its meaning is profound and beyond the grasp of our limited minds bounded by space and time. You see, we live in a temporal continuum! That's fooled you, no doubt; but never fear –

it's a new phrase I learnt recently and I have been longing to introduce it somewhere along the line. It simply means that we are subject to time; time which never stands still. There was a time when we were born, and, like it or not, there will be a time when we shall die! Any other possibility of life is not only beyond our understanding but, for the present, completely beyond our experience. We hear of differing forms of life in outer space and we still file such stories firmly under 'space fiction'. Yet the Christian faith has consistently pursued the thought that there is a form of life which is on a level completely different from that of the life we are now experiencing. This form of life is spiritual and eternal, and its source is in God, for indeed God is eternal. There was never a time when God was born and there will never be a time when God will die, for God does not live in a temporal continuum (and I bet he's pleased). He lives on the plane of life everlasting.

Therefore the answer to the question 'Who made God?' is simple – No-one! He has always been there and he always will be there. This is not only understandable but painfully logical, for is it not true that many folk get into a hopelessly illogical mess when they speak in terms of God being created by someone else? In such a situation, the next step is to say, 'Then who made that someone else?' If we reply 'X', then the next question is, 'Who made "X"?' ' Y.' 'Then who made "Y"?' And so *ad infinitum*.

> 'Big fleas have little fleas upon their backs to bite 'em,
> And little fleas have lesser fleas, and so
> *ad infinitum*.'

It is likely, at this stage, that you may feel constrained to pose a further and related question, namely, 'How do you know God is eternal? Who says?' My source of information on this point is mainly the Bible and I will be dealing with likely questions on the reliability of that book in another chapter. But it also rests on other evidence such as that for a world of the spirit and some interesting proposals from science which I introduce later in the chapter. So let us leave this for the time being and think further about the question, 'What is God really like?'

If, as already stated, no man has seen God at any time, how is it possible to know what he is like? The answer depends on the level at which your life is being lived for the present. If you live only for the passing pleasure of the moment and consider your life to be nothing more than a series of physical responses enclosed in a temporal continuum (I've done it again!), then you will no doubt find the next few pages totally incomprehensible. But if you are aware that life is not just made up of the things you can see, handle or taste, but that there are deeper aspects of life which add to it a meaning and a dimension which is difficult to assess in words, then you may begin to see something of the nature of this God, that is, what he is like.

Now I said earlier that many people's view of God was inadequate. So what sort of God would I like to have? Well surely, if he is to be a God at all, he must be able to outstrip me in all things. Without wishing to underestimate myself (modesty has always been one of my redeeming features), I hazard a guess that he would not find it too difficult to get the better of mere me. But this outlook must be taken a stage further for, as far as I am concerned, any *real* God must be able to outstrip the total of man's achievements if he is to be God at all. If it were possible for man as a whole to be able to out-think God, then our God would still be too small. But I think we must go even further than this for, as man continues to make interesting and useful discoveries, it may occur to some that he (man) might be catching up on God. Therefore it seems to me that if God is to be worth considering at all, he must in every conceivable respect not only outstrip man, but be completely beyond his grasp. It is imperative, therefore, that the God I worship should have all knowledge at his finger-tips, that he should have all power at his disposal – even if he does not choose to use it – and that he should be everywhere present.

Now it is important that you understand exactly what I am saying when I claim that the true God must be completely beyond our grasp and be able to outstrip us in all things. Let me, therefore, give you an example concerning the idea that he is everywhere present. If it were possible to find a place where God did not exist and where he could not be found, then it would be possible for me, a mere man, to escape the presence of God. But logically, this cannot be possible for the kind of God I want to worship. Wherever I go, God must be there. Should I have the ability to get me on a spaceship and fly to the farthest star, God must still be there. And if I were able to get me an oil drill and burrow my way into the depths of the earth, there he should still be with me, and his right hand should guide me. In other words, God is beyond my grasp in the sense that he is everywhere present – a state in which I could never be found. Yet in another very real sense he is completely within my grasp, indeed closer than my wife, for wherever I am, he is with me. So what is God like? He is omniscient (has all knowledge), he is omnipotent (has all power) and he is omnipresent (is everywhere present).

But this is not all. I have already propounded to you the view that my God must be eternal; that his life is lived on a plane completely different from ours, so that he is not bounded by death or the things which go to make this life rather unbearable at times. Now the idea of God being eternal or, for that matter, of anyone living for ever, is not so ridiculous as some would have us believe. I referred earlier to interesting proposals from science, and as our astronomers peer further into the outer reaches of space they are rapidly coming to the conclusion that its existence is never-ending or everlasting – an assumption which is not unreasonable if the universe has been created by an eternal God. Furthermore, some scientists have suggested that, given certain conditions, it would be possible to maintain our present form of life for an indefinite period of time. I understand that, if we were to travel in a spaceship at the speed of light, we would take some eighty-odd years to get to the nearest star and back; but because of the forces on our bodies due to the speed at which we were travelling, we would age only about the equivalent of one day. Thus, for such a journey, a pack of sandwiches would suffice for food.

Mind you, the theory is unproved and in any case the scientists have got a big problem on their hands, for how do you increase the speed of the earth to the speed of light? And assuming you were able to do this, what sort of effect would it have on us in relation to the rest of our solar system? Nonetheless, it is an interesting theory, for who would have said a thousand years ago that man would fly or go into orbit? Theoretically it was possible; after all, the birds flew! But in practice it was completely out of the question. Yet eventually both were achieved. Now if man is able to hint at the possibility of eternal life, even if the conditions are not all that desirable, surely this great God, who has all knowledge at his disposal, has well within his power the dimension of eternity and life everlasting? Does not the one follow from the other when we enlarge our vision of God? To hark back to our earlier illustration; when we are freed, even only in part, from the blindness we seem naturally to possess in relation to God, is it not painfully logical that what man can glimpse in imperfection, God can complete in perfection?

One final point as to what my God is like. He is Spirit. Now many volumes have been written on the meaning of 'Spirit' and I do not visualize myself giving a pithy summary at this stage. I merely want to suggest that it is not unreasonable to think of God in terms of Spirit, particularly if we look at man from this aspect. The Bible states that 'God made man in his own image', and one might well ask the question, 'In what sense is man the image of God?' For many, the answer is, 'In the sense of spirit.' The spirit is often described as the source of understanding, of feeling and of the will. It is, if you like, the essential 'you', what the psychologist calls the 'ego'. Our spirit makes up our personality and formulates our character, yet it would be wrong to say that the spirit *is* our character, personality, feeling, understanding and will, for it is rather the fountain from which they spring.

Evidence that we have a spirit, other than from biblical sources, is abundant, though I am in no sense advocating that we dabble too deeply in some of this evidence. I refer, of course, to involvement with the occult, an unfortunate practice which is much on the increase these days. Nonetheless, there is evidence from these sources that man is not just flesh and blood, but that he is also mind and spirit. It is from this part of man, then, that his whole being and nature springs and, as I say, many people consider that it is in his spirit that man reflects the image of God in his creation. Certainly it is in this realm that man is able to come into vital communion with God – for God is Spirit, and those who worship him must worship in spirit and truth. God then is Spirit, and because he is Spirit, he possesses all the characteristics of a person which stem from the spirit, and for this reason alone we can have the same contact with God as a person that we have with other people whom we meet day by day.

Another question about God which often bothers the genuine seeker is, 'If God is there, why does he allow all this suffering?' In order to appreciate the answer to this question it is essential to accept that God has given man the power to choose. It may be the opinion of some that this was an unwise decision on God's part, and for this reason they try to take away from man this essential characteristic, saying that he does not possess freedom of choice. But this freedom of choice is another aspect of the spirit and, while God wishes that all mankind would follow his will through communion with his Spirit, yet he does not in any sense force his way upon us, for then we would have sunk to the level of puppets and would not truly be made in the image of God. For this reason, therefore, there is much suffering in the world for which the blame must be laid firmly at man's door. Either by deliberate choice, or by sheer neglect of what he knows is right, man has allowed evil to develop unopposed and permitted wrong and suffering to continue without ever lifting a finger in protest.

On the other hand, one must freely admit that there are a number of instances where suffering has occurred which cannot in any sense be blamed on man. One has in mind natural disasters or physical illnesses which do not have their source in the foolishness of man. To tell you the truth, I have no satisfactory answer to those who question God on this count. I can assure you that you are in good company if you feel somewhat aggrieved with God for this state of affairs, for several characters in the Bible complained most bitterly to him about this same problem and the apparent injustices which they saw around them. As far as those sufferings caused by man were concerned, they did their utmost to right the wrongs they encountered. Yet on a number of occasions they were disposed, like Jeremiah, to say, 'O Lord, you have deceived me, and I was deceived!' I can say from experience that suffering tackled in the right spirit produces good, not least in the form of human maturity. But I am well aware that this is no answer to many who put this question from a heart which is genuinely aggrieved. I can only echo the words of Job, who, at a time when he had little for which to thank God, could nonetheless claim,

'I know that my Redeemer lives, and at last he will stand upon the earth.'

Below I list a number of books that you may find helpful with regard to this subject.[1] But let me make one final point on this question. When I was at school we 'did' Wordsworth, amongst other famous literary men. I was never impressed and, as a youth, claimed an almost total dislike for literature, at any rate in the form in which we tackled it. Recently, however, I visited the Lake District for my holiday and rediscovered the poet. I never even knew that he had lived in the area, let alone that his famous host of golden daffodils was beside Ullswater. We visited his home at Grasmere and as a consequence of my experience I was prompted to buy a selection of his poetry. Each evening I read a section or two and it was then that I came across this poem on suffering which summarizes so succinctly the Christian approach.

'Suffering is permanent, obscure and dark,
And has the nature of infinity.
Yet through that darkness (Infinite though it seem
And irremoveable) gracious openings lie,
By which the soul – with patient steps of thought
Now toiling, wafted now on wings of prayer –
May pass in hope, and, though from mortal bonds
Yet undelivered, rise with sure ascent
Even to the fountainhead of peace divine.'[2]

[1] Hugh Silvester, *Arguing with God* (IVP, 1971); John Eddison, *Christian Answers about Doctrine* (Scripture Union, 1966); C. S. Lewis, *The Problem of Pain* (Bles, 1940).

[2] *The King's Treasuries of Literature: Selections from Wordsworth*, edited by D. C. Somervell (Dent, reprinted 1969).

Before bringing this chapter to a conclusion, there is one other aspect of God which I should like to mention. Many who have this vague belief in some divine source are often heard to say, 'Well, it doesn't really matter which religion you have in order to find God, for they all point the same way and to the same divinity. It's just a question of emphasis, that's all.' Now I cannot see how anybody who has read even a smattering of the Bibles of other religions can come to such a conclusion, and I often wonder if this is not really some form of excuse which those concerned subconsciously erect in their minds in order to save them the trouble of finding out the truth for themselves. Let me give you just one example, though there are many others. Do you think the following quotes come from the mouth of the same God?

'Try as you may, you cannot treat all your wives impartially.'

'Good women are obedient. As for those from whom you fear disobedience, admonish them, and send them to beds apart and beat them. Then if they obey you, take no further action against them.'

'Husbands, love your wives, as Christ loved the church and gave himself up for her.'

The quotations are so contradictory that either God is a crazy mixed-up kid, or one is right and the other is wrong. I am not suggesting that it is impossible to find God in any religion other than Christianity. These religions can, for example, tell us something of the way God has shown himself in the world which he has made. But I am saying that not all who claim to reveal the true God can be said to be right. Per-

It doesn't really matter which religion ...

sonally, I am convinced that God has revealed himself supremely and this suggestion, in fact, serves to introduce us to the next chapter. It is all very well to be convinced that God is there and that he is real. But just to appreciate God as our creator and the great God of the universe is not really adequate for the complex personality of man. Surely we want to know God in a much more personal way and to feel that, great God though he may be, he is nevertheless interested in little, old unimportant me, because, you see, secretly we do not think that we are unimportant! Deep down, we think that we are the only person of note left in the universe. And you know what? That's just what God thinks as well, so let us roll to the next scene while the going is good.

4 Jesus is God

In the last two chapters you may have acquired a better understanding of God and your spiritual eyes may have been opened a small fraction. But as you have no doubt gathered, even if you come to appreciate what God is like in a very real way, he probably still appears to you as rather distant. So the question now is, 'How can we really get to know God in a vital and personal way?' You may be asking yourself how in any case did man find out about God in the first place, and who says that God is everywhere and that he knows everything? Why does he not come down to earth and show us what he is like, person to person? Then more people might believe him. These are very pertinent questions and they serve to introduce the second of our three outlooks mentioned on page 26. Mind you, with a moment's thought you would probably realize that a physical person-to-person appearance of God is out of the question, for if you were to line up just the Chinese nation in single file and get them to walk past shaking hands with you, by the time you got to the last of the 800 million or more you would be shaking hands again with the adult children of the first. Now if this is the case for just one country, how much more for the population of the whole world? So you see it is just 'not on' for God to speak with us all individually in a personal, bodily form. He can speak with us all in another sense, of course; but we will avoid complicating the issue with this thought for the time being.

If God cannot appear personally to all of us, how then, to return to the original question, did man find out about God in the first place? There are all kinds of differing views as to how religion started, some of them being in varying senses partly accurate. For example, the psychologist might say that religion in general, and God in particular, are a projection of man's mind. Man has a built-in need to worship and the 'God image' provides the authentic answer to the satisfaction of that need. Thus prayer becomes a psychological exercise giving release to the troubled mind, as does confession of sin, both activities being covered equally well by the psychiatrist when he interviews the patient in need of help.

Now it is true that religion has a psychological effect upon the worshipper. There is plenty of evidence to show that people with mental problems, and often displaying secondary physical illnesses, are 'miraculously' healed when they become Christians because their psychological problems have been solved through their new relationship with God. But this particular view fails as a full account of the source of religion, for it does away with the reality of God, assuming that he is a projection of man's mind. God becomes a mere figment of the imagination, not the supreme Being that we foreshadowed in the previous chapter.

Others see the source of religion in an evolutionary process. During the last century, and to a certain extent in this, man went mad over evolution. Every known thing or idea was re-interpreted in terms of the great Darwin's views and the origin of religion did not escape the craze. Thus some see religion developing from early animistic tendencies, such as the worship of the spirits of one's ancestors. This, it is said, gradually evolved into the worship of many different kinds of gods as man became more and more enlightened and his brain developed. Finally the process led to the worship of one God and his anthropomorphization (how's that for a good word?) in the God-Man, Jesus Christ. In one sense it is true that religion has developed. Early man's appreciation of God in the Old Testament, particularly when it comes to his moral standards, shows quite a backward outlook in comparison with the New Testament idea of God as seen in the standards of Christ. But to suggest that man by his own efforts was able gradually to discover the truth about God leads automatically to an unanswerable question. If this is so, what guarantee have we got that 'man' is right in his assessment of the situation?

A third view concerning the origin of religion sees God as an extremely useful 'idea' on the part of the State. In order that the authorities might have some form of backing for their laws and customs which would appeal to the peasants, it was necessary to invent a supreme Being who gave his tacit approval to all the whims and fancies of the monarch. Thus, if he felt like having five wives when everybody else was allowed only one, it was necessary to support his behaviour by claiming a divine revelation for his action, either directly to himself, or through a priest of his choosing. We see an example of the State ordering of divinities in the early days of Christianity when the authorities claimed the right to decide what gods might be worshipped. There were even laws which said no-one should have gods apart from the State and that all new gods had to be 'registered', as it were, to obtain legal recognition. Christians never saw their way clear to obtaining such recognition and, in consequence, there were frequent conflicts with the State's view of religion.

Contrary to the above views, the major religions of the world claim that, on his own, man was unable to discover the truth about God and that it needed God himself to tell man what it was all about before he could have even the faintest idea of God. This, basically, is what the Bible claims. Now I freely acknowledge that there is a definite difference of opinion as to whose revelation of God is right, and I have already hinted at a possible solution to this problem in the last chapter.[1] My advice is to read the various revelations for yourself and come to your own conclusion. There is, however, a better and quicker way than that – one which I shall be putting to you in the next chapter. In brief it is, 'The proof of the pudding is in the eating', or 'God helps those who help themselves', as one thief said to the other. Meanwhile, let us continue with our consideration of the idea that God has shown himself to us in a definite way.

Now there is no point in beating about the bush, for I am sure that most of you will already have come to the conclusion that I am about to launch out on a theological treatise about the nature of Jesus Christ. To a certain extent, though not altogether, you are right. Let us hark back to our view of God in the previous chapter. For a moment just try to

[1] See pp. 40–41.

picture in your mind who this divine Being really is. I reminded you of the immense power at his disposal (it amazes me why he does not strike us all dead on the spot: perhaps he has a reason for it – who knows?), the amazing knowledge which he possesses, his availability in all places, the 'other' realms in which he lives. How could such a Being tell us something about himself in a way that we could understand? If he appeared to us in super-human form (you know, rather like Batman), we would probably not recognize him as true to life. If he appeared to us in a dazzling show of his might and power, we should probably not survive the onslaught. Yet if God is who he is, how else could we find out about him other than by revelation?

Some people make God out to be rather complicated; but when dealing with man he is always simple. You see, like all good teachers, God starts with the premise that his pupils, to put it mildly, are somewhat reluctant to learn. Now he has got a problem on his hands – how to convince these indifferent pupils that he is God. What better solution than to become a human like one of them? For if, despite his cloak of humanity, his true divinity could shine through, then indeed he would be able to tell them something about himself.

Now this is just what he did: he emptied himself, and took upon himself the form of a man, and that man is Jesus Christ. Have you noticed how Christ's name is on everybody's lips today, though usually in a form of reproach rather than in any appreciative sense? It is strange, don't you think, that the people who claim that they do not believe in Christ frequently use his name as an oath? Now I am not as squeamish as some of my Christian brethren when it comes to the use of words and phrases, but the use of Christ's name as an oath really turns me over. This is because, for the genuine Christian, Christ is more than just a human name; it is the name which tells us of very God himself. In the early days of Christianity a believer was tested in the matter of his faith by being asked to state that 'Jesus is Lord'. If he could say that, particularly when the monarch wanted him to say 'The Emperor is Lord', then his faith must be real.

But I can hear some of you saying, 'How, then, do we *know* that Jesus is God come down to earth in the form of a man?' Well, there are a number of answers to this question. I could put on my intellectual cloak and start to demonstrate to you how the historians have shown that Christ was in every sense a real historical figure. I could parade before your eyes the convincing evidence there is for the historicity of Christ. But many have done all this before me, and with greater skill.[2] Yet even were you to read all the volumes of information there are on these points, you would still not necessarily be convinced that Jesus is God, even if you felt he was truly historical. Nevertheless, in order to give you some sort of guide-lines for the answer to this question, let me put just two considerations before you. I think Jesus was real because he was down to earth (and I am not trying to be funny). He behaved as I would expect God to behave; yet he behaved in a way which I, simple fool that I am, can understand and appreciate. For a start he harpooned the hypo-

[2] See, for example, chapter one of Sir Norman Anderson's book, *Christianity: the witness of history* (IVP, 1969).

crites. If you feel that it is a justifiable argument against religion to say that all church-goers are hypocrites, then you read what Jesus had to say about them. He would agree with you, though he would probably question your use of the word 'all'. But he did not mince his words. 'You generation of vipers', he said, 'whited sepulchres all of you.' Do you know what a whited sepulchre is? Well, never mind; it's rather a long story. But it would have the same sort of effect on the hypocrites of Christ's day as calling the Conservative leader a Communist might have today. So with one breath he strips the religious leaders of their thin disguise of holiness, and with another he helps the prostitutes to leave their ill-gotten gains. He even claims that they have more chance of heaven than the Pharisees – and I bet that upset them. You see, Jesus did not come to help those who thought they were all right; he came to help those who knew they were all wrong. You often hear people saying, 'I will worship God when I am a bit better.' But that is hypocrisy. God wants you as you are, not as you think you are or could be.

The second consideration I put to you is this. You cannot sit on the fence when it comes to Jesus Christ. Either he is a crank or else he is God. He said, 'Whoever believes in me will not perish but have everlasting life.' What arrogance! Unless it is true! He claimed to be God; 'I and my Father are one,' he said. Only a fool would claim to be God unless he is God! And who but God would put up with thick-skinned individuals such as Simon Peter and even make him a leader; who but God would introduce moral standards which man is totally incapable of keeping even in part, despite all his

You cannot sit on the fence

modern inventions? We find these moral standards in the Sermon on the Mount and on one occasion my barber said to me (that is, when I used to go to the barber's!), 'You know, I believe it is right to keep the Sermon on the Mount, but you take God far too seriously. You know, all this church business.' 'Oh', I said, with a certain measure of disbelief in his claim. 'Do you mean to tell me that you've never thought of having sex with a woman other than your wife?' He was baffled for a minute and said, 'Why, is that in the Sermon on the Mount?' It is, as I am sure you know. However, he thought he had got me when he replied, 'And what about you, then?' 'Ah,' I said, 'the difference between your standard and mine is that you think you're good when you're a sinner, whereas I know I'm a sinner and need God's help.'

Beverley Nichols, when looking at the question of Jesus as God, said in reply to the radical French scholar, Professor Guignebert,

'... all he will admit, in his most generous moment, is that "the outline of a man and the traces of an individual activity are still to be distinguished".

'Ye gods! If you have ever done any writing you may have a faint idea of the immense difficulty of making a character *live* even for a single publishing season, in a single language. And if you have ever done any reading ... you (will know) that there are no "characters" ... which are more than tiny shadows against the immense reality of the character of Jesus.

'You cannot deny the reality of this character, *in whatever body it resided*. Even if we were to grant the Professor's theory that it is all a hotch-potch of legend, *somebody* said "The Sabbath was made for man, and not man for the Sabbath"; *somebody* said "For what shall it profit a man if he shall gain the whole world and lose his own soul"; ... *somebody* said "How hardly shall they that have riches enter into the Kingdom of God" ...

'*Somebody* said these things.... And whoever said them was *gigantic*. And whoever said them was *living*, ... and yet we cannot find in any contemporary literature any phrases which have a shadow of the beauty, the truth, the individuality, nor the *indestructibility* of those phrases.'[3]

God is clear – when you see him in Jesus Christ. Read the New Testament in a modern version. I would suggest J.B. Phillips or the Revised Standard Version or the *Good News Bible*. If you do this and read with the honesty I suggested in the first chapter, then indeed will your vision of God be much increased, for you will see him as he intended you to see him. Not in all his beauty, because you could never stand that any more than I could. But you will see just as much as God wants you to see; and whatever that is, I can assure you, you will not be disappointed.

[3] Quoted from Beverley Nichols, *The Fool Hath Said* (Cape, 1936), pp. 126f. (Nichols' italics) by Leon Morris in *The Lord from heaven* (IVP, 1958, 2nd edition, 1974), pp. 15f.

5 The proof of the pudding...

So where are we? We reckon that God is around, even if our picture of him is a little dim. We have come to the conclusion that we shall get a better picture of God if we look at Jesus Christ and the only way we can do that is to read all about him in the Bible, particularly the New Testament. Let us assume that we have done all this and that we are convinced beyond all shadow of doubt that he is real. Where does this get us? The answer is, nowhere!

You may be thinking, 'Well, surely, if I were convinced that God and Jesus Christ are real, then I *would* believe.' No! I do not think you would, if you did not want to believe. You see, there is a writer in the Bible by the name of James (no relation!) and he says, 'You have faith enough to believe that there is one God. Excellent! The devils have faith like that, and it makes them tremble.' Now I agree that that is not a very polite thing to say about the glimpse of light you have received so far. But do not forget that we are being honest with ourselves, and it is no good my saying that, if you believe in God, you will be all right, when I know full well you will not be all right. So far, you have not even arrived at an equivalent view of God that the devils hold, for I am fairly certain that, as you read this book, few if any of you are sitting there trembling! At least the devils have the decency to tremble at the thought of God. Do not worry too much about this trembling business, however, for the devils are shaking because they are afraid of God, knowing what he will be doing to them in the not-too-distant future. But no such fear need grip you. The genuine believer in God has no need to be afraid of him, for God is love, and there is no fear in love, for perfect love casts out fear.

But for the moment, maybe, you would not class yourself as a genuine believer, so the question still remains, 'How do we really get to know God?' The answer is by personal experience, and this introduces the third aspect that I said we would tackle back on page 26. Now this phrase 'personal experience' needs a deal of clarification and in this chapter and the next I intend to attempt a clearing of the muddy waters. Basically, however, this outlook is the foundation of the answer to a genuine encounter with God.

Here an example to illustrate my point may help, even if it is a negative one. Many moons ago I persuaded my wife to grow her hair long. Being a dutiful wife, and knowing that I liked her hair that way, she did! But, needless to say, there came a time when she wanted to do a Delilah on herself and cut it all off. Now I did not like this thought at all, so I threatened that, if she cut her hair, I would grow a beard, knowing, of course, that that was something she certainly would not wish me to do. For some time the *status quo* existed until one Saturday we chanced to be shopping in Debenhams (we reckon on charging the firm a fee for this unintentional advert!). There on a stand were a load of wigs which

55

made an Indian war-dance pale into insignificance. One by one we tried them on – at least Ann tried them on – and, sure enough, the inevitable happened. We chanced across a wig of short hair that was just her colour. Against my better judgment no doubt, I persuaded her to buy it. Next day the wig was worn in church, which is the usual place to parade one's new acquisitions, as I'm sure you will appreciate. Of course the womenfolk, and even some of the men, commented on her short hair, how nice it looked and so on. But the truth will out and with the passage of time they discovered that it was all a sham. She still looks nice in the wig, mind you – but it was not her own hair. Her short hair had been put to the test and found wanting.

Now, like my wife's wig, your vision of God is, at the moment, a bit artificial. It is real in the sense that you understand something about him, just as the wig is a real and material article. But your vision of God is artificial in the sense that it has no lasting and personal effect upon your life and actions, in the same way that a wig is not a real part of the person wearing it. But once you know the presence of God personally in your life, then for you he is a reality. And coupled with a genuine faith you will have a real and permanent experience of God which no-one will be able to shake. Now I would suggest that you cannot have a true and personal encounter with God until you make an effort to meet him. So, then, how do we obtain this personal experience of God?

The first thing is to start looking in the right place. Jesus said, 'Seek, and you will find; knock, and it will be opened to you.' The trouble is that many people are looking in the wrong place, and listening with the wrong ears. Not so long ago scientists were saying that fish did not communicate with each other. Man, you see, with characteristic empiricism, had stuck his head underneath the water and, since he did not hear anything, came to the conclusion that there was nothing to hear. But, as is often the case, he was wrong! True, with the human ear he could hear nothing; but with a highly-sensitive microphone and all the necessary clap-trap of equipment to go with it, he discovered that the fish made a lot of noise. You may think that God never speaks to you. But I would say you are wrong, for he has been shouting at you for years. Your trouble has been that you have not been in the right place, or on the right wavelength, or in the right frame of mind to hear him. So let us see if we can get ourselves into this right frame of mind, shall we?

Most of us have got a pretty high opinion of ourselves, and why not? After all, we are better than old short-ears across the road; he fiddles his income tax, I am sure (I think it has got something to do with lump sums!). And Mr Harlequin Longbottom, called 'Botters' for short, has got a bit on the side up in Shirley, and we would never do that, would we? Yes, I am sure that, as we look around, we can find many whom we surpass in excellence.

But how about comparing ourselves with God for a moment? You remember we said we could find out a bit more about God by looking at Jesus Christ? Then, like my barber, let us take the Sermon on the Mount for starters. I bet you would like to be in old Botters' place, but you lack the guts. Jesus said in the Sermon, 'If a man looks on a woman with a lustful eye, he has already committed adultery with her in his heart.' Are you really any better than Botters? And then there is old short-ears. My! You would like to catch him out, wouldn't you? How it angers you that he can get away with it and have his colour telly, not to mention his two cars, while you cannot get away with anything because your tax is stopped at source. Jesus said in the Sermon, 'Anyone who nurses anger against his brother (neighbour) must be brought to judgment.' Then those of you who think you are holy and go to church to parade your good works for all to see, you think that this is what God really wants. But this is what Jesus said in the Sermon, 'Be careful not to make a show of your religion before men.' And so I could go on – but you read the words of Jesus for yourself in Matthew chapters 5 and 6.

Now I hasten to add that I am not setting myself up as a paragon of virtue. Far from it! I am trying, on the contrary, to introduce you to a shaft of light that will either break you or make you. Until now we have had only the occasional glimpse of God and his dazzling brilliance. But now we are beginning to see him as he really is, for the more we look at God, and compare ourselves with him, the more we realize what a sorry state we have arrived at in our own lives. To compare ourselves with others is easy. There must be some who are worse than us. But to compare ourselves with God as revealed to us by Jesus Christ brings us inevitably to one conclusion: we just fall far short of his standard, for his standard is perfection. There are many things, you see, which blind us and prevent us from seeing ourselves as we really are. I have touched on some of them already, such as our religious pride, our anger and our lust, to mention but a few. But if we are genuinely honest with ourselves and are prepared to acknowledge these faults in our lives, then some of the mud can be cleared so that we can get a better vision of God and perhaps hear something of what he is saying. To use our earlier phrase, we will be able to have a real experience of God.

Back in the nineteenth century, during the era of cabin-boys, holds and sailing-ships, a particular Captain was being given rather too much cheek by his spotty-faced lad. Wishing to teach him a lesson, he decided to put him into the empty, rat-infested hold, thinking that such an experience would soon calm him down. Some time after he had battened down the hatches he was surprised to hear derisive songs coming from the hold about certain types of ladies who were coming down from somewhere in Scotland (he did not quite catch the place). This puzzled him at first, that is, that the lad was not worried about being in the hold – the ladies from Scotland are another story altogether! But then he hit on a brilliant idea. He would suspend a lamp in the hold and see what difference that made. Sure enough, within a few minutes the lad was crying for mercy, imploring the Captain to release him, for now that light had been introduced, he realized what a terrible place he was in. Before that the darkness had blinded him and he had assumed all was well; but now he saw that he was surrounded by filth, rags and rats. What is more, he could see that the light was only partially revealing his condition, for there were nooks and crannies on the other side of the hold where the light did not penetrate. Yet it was sufficient to suggest to him that these other areas contained horrors even worse than those within his immediate reach.

The same applies to us and God. As we gradually begin to appreciate what God is like, and as his light begins to cast a chink across our lives, then we begin to realize what a state we are in and slowly we come to make a more accurate assessment of our situation and nature. Perhaps we are not so great after all. Things which we thought were all right were, in fact, all wrong. Indeed, even some of the things which we did as acts of kindness seem to have a tinge of dirt about them. For we helped old Mother Crabtree only because we knew she had got a lot stacked away, or so they said. At the time we would have vehemently denied it; but now, as God's light sheds a ray across our path, we are beginning to see the truth about our so-called acts of kindness. And what about those dark corners of our minds, those vague suggestions that have flitted through our thought-processes but never seen the light of day? Oh, we would never do that! Or would we?

Now the Bible never minces words; it calls all this *sin*. And when we realize this, then we are ready to receive a more personal encounter with God. Indeed we have already begun the process of getting better acquainted with him, for we have begun to see something of what he is like. But we are still human, and which one of us really likes to admit that we have done wrong? We go into all sorts of contortions in order to convince ourselves and others that we are not too bad on the whole. We can deceive other people quite easily, but God we can never deceive. He knows exactly what we are like. He has told us so in the

Bible. Read Romans 3 for an aperitif, and the book of Amos for a main course, particularly chapter 6. There is only one answer as far as God is concerned, and that is to say we are sorry. Of course, there are different ways of being sorry. With great glee, the little toad at school trips up his friend in the corridor and is just about to gloat over his victim when he spies the Deputy Head approaching with all systems go. 'Sorry,' he says, 'I didn't mean to do it.' The little liar! He had every intention of doing it. The only reason for his apparent change of outlook was the possible threat of retribution from the fast-approaching Deputy. This kind of sorrow is total hypocrisy and completely alien to God's view of what is required. So what sort of sorrow might he be looking for?

Some years ago, I whiled away a couple of years in the Royal Air Force, 'doing' my National Service. One of the many jobs of that enforced vacation was called 'square-bashing'. In our particular flight we had a nice, softly-spoken gentleman called a Corporal who would, periodically, take us for little walks on a nearby large playground. Having arrived at our destination he would set us marching across the tarmac, which was a good half-mile in length. While striding across this vast desert we would have an excellent view of row upon row of neat Nissen huts. Each was exactly spaced and separated by weed-free paths lined with stones painted the inevitable white. Here and there the odd Spitfire stood with nonchalant air, just to remind us that we were still in the RAF. Drinking in this idyllic scene our sense of euphoria would be suddenly broken by the dulcet tones of the aforesaid Corporal who was asking us,

A nice, softly-spoken gentleman

in a language that appeared foreign, if we would be good enough to turn about. Being obedient airmen we acquiesced – not only that, we did as he said. And now the scene was completely different. Instead of the huts, of which enough has been said already, there stretched out before us the rolling hills of Cannock Chase, and as the ever-receding folds disappeared into a sun-drenched mist you could almost imagine that you saw the Holy City, the New. . . . 'Airman! What the (censored) do you think you're doing?' And once again we were brought down to earth after visions of rapture tinged with thoughts of possible escape.

The point of all this is that, while on the parade-ground, our view had been completely altered. Instead of revolting and ugly man-made Nissen huts, we saw something of the beauties that God had to offer. And this is what God requires of us. Instead of concentrating all our efforts on the dross and emptiness of this life with all its frivolities – not necessarily wrong in themselves, but sufficient to distract our attention from God – he wants us to make a right-about turn and direct our attention towards him, so that we can see more of the possibilities of life that he has to offer. In short, he wants us to change our whole attitude towards him. Instead of being against him, we are for him; instead of trying to deceive him (if that were possible), we are completely open with him, telling him in very truth our own deficiencies; instead of hating him, we love him; instead of cursing him, we ask him to bless us; instead of delighting in sin, we turn our back on sin and follow the light which God sheds on our path.

Jesus had a word for all this. He called it 'repentance'. Indeed, his first recorded words in Mark's Gospel are, 'The time is fulfilled, and the kingdom of God is at hand; repent, and believe in the gospel.' We will be thinking more about this phrase the 'kingdom of God', or 'kingdom of heaven', in due course, but for the time being let us not forget that our question is, 'How do we really get to know God?' Well, Jesus himself suggests that one thing we need to do is to change our attitude towards him; that is, repent. But then he goes on to say, '. . . believe'. Now that is not so easy. How can you believe in something you have not seen, and how can you believe in something you cannot prove? Well, of course, by the very definition of the word 'believe', to 'see' and 'prove' would mean we have no need to believe! But I fully appreciate the difficulty, so let me give you an example.

If you are in the habit of catching buses (and I hope for your sake you are not), before you get on board you do not expect the driver to give you a run-down on how the engine works, neither do you expect evidence that the bus has been properly maintained. What is more, when the bus conductor tells you that the vehicle is going to the railway station, you do not ask him to prove it – he can't, anyway! Yet by stepping on to the bus and accepting the ride from the Company, you exercise faith in at least three directions. First, you are trusting in a device you do not fully understand – the engine. Secondly, you do not know the bus is roadworthy – you trust the Company to maintain it so (and sometimes they let you down). Finally, you have no proof that the bus will reach its destination – you trust the driver and conductor to honour their stated objectives. This is the kind of trust that Jesus asks of us. It is not blind optimism any more than getting on a bus is blind optimism (though some might think so!). It is faith in a person who, unlike the Bus Company, will never let you down.

You may well ask, 'Trust in Jesus for what?' And the answer is bound up in the words quoted above. Jesus said the kingdom of God is near, and by that he meant that God's rule as King in our hearts and lives could be a reality for those who wanted it, that is for those who believed. This was the 'good news' or the gospel that he came to proclaim. But there is a lot more to it than these few lines would suggest. Nonetheless, when we change our attitude towards him and trust him, then he is able to enter into every aspect of our lives and with our co-operation he brings his standards to bear on our everyday experiences. In other words, he rules in our lives – literally. You see, we have now got a different view of God. Instead of the Nissen huts, we see the rolling hills; instead of being opposed to God, we want to please him, not because he says so, but because we love him, and we want to serve him as any good subject would want to serve his king.

So then, your side in this business of getting to know God is repentance and faith. But perhaps we have put the cart before the horse, for the more important aspect is what God has done for us. The light is slowly dawning upon us and the mists on the far-off hills are beginning to clear (though they never did in Cannock Chase – too many coal-mines, you know). But it is not until we discover and appreciate what God has done for us in Jesus Christ that we can really begin to know something of the rule of God in our lives. So, in answering the question, 'Trusting Jesus for what?', let us in this next chapter forget ourselves for a moment and see if God has done anything for us which demands our allegiance.

6 ... is in the eating

One of the many spin-offs of trusting in God is that a number of the problems about which other people tend to worry need not bother us, for we can safely leave them in God's capable hands. Mind you, a number of different problems are likely to come our way which may not have bothered us before, so it probably evens out in the long run. But there was one big problem which God had on his mind about which none of us could do a thing, and in looking at this problem we will be answering the question, 'For what are we trusting God?'

The book of Genesis tells us that, after God had finished remoulding the earth and creating man, he sat down and admired his handiwork, coming to the conclusion that it was 'very good'. In fact, God gave himself ten out of ten and with a hearty good pat on the back lay down to rest for a while. Everything in the garden was lovely, if you get my meaning! But then along comes this serpent, the cunning devil, and spoils it all. And when he had finished, man had become sinful and death lurked at the door. 'Dust thou art, and unto dust shalt thou return,' said the older version of the Bible.

Now I would suggest that you avoid getting bogged down at this stage in all the arguments as to whether or not the story is history, parable, myth, legend and all that jazz, for this can be just another cunning device of that very same serpent to guide your mind away from the truth of the story, which is that man sinned and with sin came death. For this is where God's problem comes in, you see. To begin with, he had made everything perfect; but now all that had gone. So what should he do? One thing was true for sure; man could not raise himself from the dead. You try it and see. Mind you, man has been trying to deal with the other problem, the one of sin, for quite a long time, but not very successfully, if we are honest with ourselves. In any case, God knows that man cannot succeed in this either, for while we do not sin constantly all the time, we nonetheless have within us a natural inclination to do wrong instead of right. You put four men and one woman on a desert island where there is hardly enough food for one and see how they will love one another – not to mention other things. So God had to work out how to get rid of these twin problems of sin and death; and this is how he did it.

First of all he gave man a law to keep, but he just could not manage it. Poor old Moses! He got quite uptight about it all because the Israelites broke God's law even when the finger of God was still hot upon the tablet. Basically, you see, this law was to be found in the Ten Commandments and it could be conveniently divided into two parts. The first four commandments suggested the duty we should show towards God, while the last six told us how we should treat our neighbour. 'There is only one God to worship,' said the first commandment. 'And you know how great he is,' said the second, 'so don't make any image of him.' 'Reverence his name and character,' said the third; 'and don't forget to worship him on the sabbath day,' insisted the fourth. With such an almighty God in mind what else could we do but treat our neighbour right? 'So honour mummy and daddy,' said the fifth; 'and respect a person's life,' the sixth demanded; 'not to mention his wife,' replied the seventh. 'Oh! And don't walk off with things that aren't yours,' said the eighth. 'And always tell the whole truth,' the ninth insisted. And to sum it all up – 'Watch what goes on in your mind, for that's where all the trouble starts.'

Well, can you imagine their keeping all that lot? Of course not. You would have to be perfect to behave like that, wouldn't you? So time and time again they broke his commandments, and you can see why, really. You read through the list in Exodus 20 and see if you measure up to the standard. There were occasions when some of the people realized that they were not coming up to scratch and, when they turned to God in faith and repentance, he forgave them. Take David for an example of God's forgiveness. He took a fancy to Bathsheba, Uriah's wife. Mind you, she was flaunting herself; but David knew God's standard and there was no excuse really. After they had committed adultery he got rid of her old man by putting him in the front line when the next battle came along, which was tantamount to murder. In the end David and Bathsheba paid dearly for their sin; but David repented and God forgave him.

Nonetheless, this plan of God's in giving man a set of rules to live by was not working out too well. But he was not taken by surprise, for he had already devised another idea which he had worked out right from the very beginning. He was just waiting for the right time to introduce it and that came a little under 1,980 years ago. If men could not get themselves out of their own mess even with a list of God's rules, then the only solution was for God to come down to earth and pull them out of the mire himself. Man's sin had brought death. But if God could take that punishment for sin upon himself, then man could be freed from the penalty of sin, always assuming, of course, that this was what he (man) wanted. So he arrived; and they called his name Jesus, because he would 'save his people from their sins'. And as Jesus himself said, he came 'not to be served but to serve, and to give his life as a ransom for many'. So on that dark and dismal day some thirty years after his birth, Christ gave up his life voluntarily, and they laid him in a tomb. But God raised him from the dead, a fact to which many people were witnesses. And the purpose of it all? A fellow called Paul sums it up like this, 'Let it be known to you therefore, ... that through this man forgiveness of sins is proclaimed to you, and by him every one that believes is freed from everything from which you could not be freed by the law of Moses.'

Perhaps you can see now a shaft of light, which, if you understand it, must be dazzling in the extreme. For if what I have recorded above is true, then the repentance and faith which we have towards Jesus Christ brings to us forgiveness of sins. For one thing is certain: we shall never be able to free ourselves from sin by trying to keep the law. But you know this introduces a second and even more important thing that God has done for us in this action of Christ on the cross, one which has been sadly neglected for a

Even with a list of God's rules

long time in modern Christianity but is just as important as his act of forgiveness.

God's problem went a bit deeper than just forgiving us for all the wrong things we had done. True, he wanted to forgive us, but that was not all. He wanted also to restore us to the position with him in creation that he had originally intended for man before that cunning old devil came along – a position of perfection and everlasting life. But how could he do that, for we have already seen that everybody sins and falls short of the standard which God sets for us? Well, you see, when Christ sacrificed his life on the cross, he not only made it possible for our sins to be forgiven. He also made it possible for us to be counted as righteous in God's eyes.

Now who on earth wants to be righteous today, for the word suggests a prig or a snob, doesn't it? This is a pity, really, for the dictionary defines the word as 'upright' or, more to the point, 'law-abiding'. Now God wants us to be law-abiding, that is to keep his law. So it was that, when he died on the cross, he also made it possible for us to be counted as law-abiding. 'How did he do that?' you may well ask. Well, Christ had not broken God's law; he was already righteous or law-abiding. Yet he was receiving a punishment of death reserved only for those who *had* broken God's law. In other words, he was receiving the punishment which should really have been ours. But then, because in his own right he was already law-abiding, death could not hold him. So, when the sacrifice on the cross was complete, he was raised from the dead to prove that he himself is righteous and that he is able to count as righteous all those who have faith in him.

Let me put it another way. However much we try to be good and please this almighty God whose light is beginning to dazzle us in a rather frightening way, we shall never succeed. For even if we were to be perfect from now on, there are all our sins of the past still to be reckoned against us. But God does not ask us to try to be righteous, or law-abiding, by keeping a set of rules. Instead, he says he will give us his own righteousness to wear in rather the same way as we put on a coat. Thus we shall be 'counted' as righteous, providing we have faith in the sacrifice of Jesus on the cross for the forgiveness of our sins, and trust in his resurrection as the guarantee that we are indeed counted righteous by God.

'Yippee!' I can hear some pervert shouting. 'So we can go and have a grand orgy and afterwards all we have to do is to ask for forgiveness and all will be well, because God has counted those of us who believe as righteous?' Nothing can be further from the truth. Does faith do away with the law and make it useless? By no means. On the contrary, the true believer will want to keep the law, not because he has to, or because he feels he ought to out of a sense of duty, but because he loves with an everlasting love the Saviour who was prepared to go all this way to restore him once again to a right relationship with God. You see, we are counted as righteous by God through his undeserved kindness; it comes to us as a free gift acceptable by faith. We have done nothing at all to earn this gift from God. As a consequence we have nothing about which to boast. No principle of 'doing things' on our part has brought us this peace with God. Only this principle of faith, for a man is counted righteous by faith, not by the actions of keeping the law.

Let us have a recap, so that we can get clear in our minds exactly what I am telling you. Originally God made man perfect. But once man had sinned he brought death upon himself, and now we all naturally tend towards sin rather than righteousness. If you like, the wages that we earn for sin is death. God, who is wholly righteous, comes to earth as a man and receives a punishment for sin which he has not committed. He gives his life as a ransom for many; he pays the wages of man's sin himself. Thus all who wish to accept his offer may be forgiven their sins. But death comes only to those who sin by nature, and God's nature is that of righteousness. Because of this latter fact, it follows that Jesus did not remain in the grave for long. Indeed, he rose from the dead, so that all who believe could have the righteousness of Christ placed upon them like a coat, a righteousness which is totally undeserved on the part of man. He has done nothing to earn it; yet it is a free gift which God is only too willing to pass over to any who genuinely repent and believe in the sacrifice of Christ. Now when a man is clothed with God's righteousness, God is able to offer him another gift. He is able, in fact, to return man to his original state and give him eternal life. And this is indeed the sure and certain promise that Christ has given us, that those who believe will not perish but have everlasting life. Just as Christ rose from the dead, so all those who believe will be raised up to everlasting life.

This, then, is the amazing grace which God has made conspicuous for us in Jesus Christ, for grace means 'undeserved kindness'. He, 'who was put to death for our sins and raised for our justification', offers everything we could possibly ask for – as a *free gift*. I have not used this word 'justification' before, but it means 'counted righteous' or 'counted law-abiding' and it is a word you will come across frequently in the Bible.[1] Another way of putting it is to say that justification means 'just as if I'd never sinned'. Perhaps now you are beginning to see the significance of our title, for God 'makes just' or 'counts as righteous' all those who believe in him. But I wonder if this final shaft of light is too bright for you? Perhaps, like Paul in the New Testament when he first faced up to the light of Jesus Christ, you are blinded with a combination of amazement on the one hand and unbelief on the other. Well, Paul's blindness was only temporary; and maybe after a few days, as you think about the contents of these last two chapters, the wonder of it all will gradually dawn upon you and you will begin to see how this life of faith brings to you the very benefits which you have always been seeking but which have ever been beyond your grasp.

Let us start to assess some of these benefits. First of all, since we have been counted as righteous by faith, we now have peace with God through our Lord Jesus Christ. No longer are we separated from God by the barrier of our sin. Our sinful nature is still there, as we shall see later; but it is no longer a barrier to our friendship with God because we are counted righteous through faith. Whatever the struggles, arguments, strikes, famines and disagreements which may be going on around us, we shall not be moved by these from our confident relationship and

[1] See also Robert M. Horn, *Go free!* (IVP, 1976).

friendship with Christ and the inner peace which he gives. Mind you, they will affect us outwardly. If we are involved in a disagreement it may upset us. Perhaps we were partly responsible and will need to take some action to make amends for our lack of good will. But these things will not affect our peace with God so long as we always relate our whole life with all its many activities to Jesus Christ. In fact, because we are justified, we shall accept difficulty, not in the sense of naïvely inviting trouble by a false religious charade, but because we know that the troubles that surround us train us to persevere in our faith and that this perseverance brings proof that our justification has stood the test of life's difficulties.

Furthermore, there are two other immediate consequences which this justification brings to us. One is that God's love has been poured into our hearts. Now the effect of this upon our life is dynamic, for through love we are able to start practising the whole law of God, not because we have got to, out of a sense of duty, but because we want to from the depths of our heart. It is the least we can do in response to the grace which God has shown us. 'Love God with all your heart, soul, mind and strength,' said Jesus; and this we can do, for through faith his love has been (not will be) poured into our hearts. 'Love your neighbour as yourself,' continued Jesus; and what else can we do when, through faith, God's love has been literally 'poured' into our hearts? Of course, it will not be easy. We shall need God's strength to help us. But, as long as we realize this, then, when we do succeed in loving our neighbour, we have nothing to boast about, for it is God's love working through us. It is in this sense that we are able, as we were saying earlier, to keep the law through our faith. We thus find that, whatever our circumstances, we are increasingly able to cope with them. Indeed, we do not just cope with them, but eventually overcome them, because through faith in Christ his love in us reaches out to the unlovely – the business associate who is doing us down, the neighbour who throws his rubbish over our fence, the pupil who knows no control, the friend who deserts us.

But how is God's love poured into our hearts? 'God's love has been poured into our hearts through the Holy Spirit which has been given to us,' and this is the second immediate consequence of our justification. When we have faith in Christ for forgiveness of sins and justification, we receive the very Spirit of God himself. It is not something which we will receive later, nor is it something of which we will receive a proportion now, followed by much more at a later time. Paul made it quite clear that, 'since we are justified by faith, we have peace with God through our Lord Jesus Christ', and his love is in our hearts through the Holy Spirit 'which has been given to us', not 'will be given to us'. His coming into our lives is a once-for-all event, received as a gift (we cannot earn it by any means) when first we genuinely believe.

Peter records in Acts 11 how he received the Holy Spirit as a free gift from God when he first believed in the Lord Jesus Christ. He is giving an account to the church leaders in Jerusalem of his behaviour at the house of Cornelius. In verse 15 he describes how the Holy Spirit fell on those first Gentile believers and in verse 16 he links their experience unequivocally (without a doubt, so to speak) with the words of

Christ at the ascension, just prior to Pentecost, concerning the promise that the disciples would be baptized with the Holy Spirit. In the story of the ascension, in the first chapter of Acts, Jesus says that they will be baptized with the Holy Spirit in a few days, and it is safe to assume that he is referring to the coming Day of Pentecost which is described in the next chapter. Then in Acts 11:17 Peter makes it abundantly clear that this gift of the baptism of the Holy Spirit which they received at Pentecost was also the time when they believed on the Lord Jesus Christ, that is, the time when they first became justified Christians. The whole incident is then linked in verses 17 and 18 with the occasion when the Gentiles, in the form of Cornelius' household, first came to believe on the Lord Jesus Christ. So then, the moment we believe in Christ for justification, we receive the gift of his Holy Spirit.

I would like to end this chapter on a cautionary note. Do not imagine that, because you are counted as righteous or law-abiding by God through your faith in Christ, you have therefore been *made* righteous. This is far from the case. Indeed the likelihood is that, now that the love of God has been poured into your heart, you will suddenly realize that much of what you considered as good and honest before you met with Christ is in fact very far from good and decidedly dishonest. It has been rightly said that the difference between a Christian and a non-Christian is that a Christian knows he is a sinner and is prepared to acknowledge it, whereas a non-Christian thinks he is righteous. Your natural inclination to sin is still within you and, because God's love and his Holy Spirit are within you as well, this sinful nature will tend to stand out like a sore thumb by contrast. But do not let this worry you, for it will keep you humble. As you see God's love working out in your life and reaching others, you will never be tempted to boast of your good works, for you know that nothing good dwells within you naturally.

Finally I must point out that you will find much of what I have said in this chapter in Romans 3 – 8. In one sense it is not easy reading, but this book may have helped you to untie the knot. In another sense it is extremely simple, for even a child can understand it. Basically the message is this: provided we humble ourselves before God and ask his forgiveness for our sin; provided we trust in Christ's death and resurrection to bring us forgiveness on the one hand and God's righteousness on the other; then we can have the love of God together with his Holy Spirit poured into our hearts and lives. What more can a person want, to see his way through this life – and the next?

7 A bed of roses?

There is a brand of Christianity which often gives the unsuspecting recruit the impression that all you have to do is to 'come to Jesus' and your troubles will be solved. There is a sense in which this is true, in that faith, your faith which you now have in the risen Lord, can look ahead with a sure and certain hope to that day when God will fulfil his promise and you will share with him his glory in a life that is everlasting. The wonder and majesty of this future hope which he has already grasped by faith is something which never ceases to thrill the genuine Christian. It is described in the Bible with a mixture of symbol, parable and literal truth and has caused many to stumble in their trust in Christ. But to those who read with the eye of faith, possessing the love of Christ and the Holy Spirit within, it presents them with an assurance of the presence and power of Christ which nothing on earth can shake. Having this confidence that nothing will ever separate us from the love of God for the rest of eternity, we can indeed say that all our problems are solved.

But in terms of our present life here, with our feet firmly placed on the ground, such a statement is far from the truth. As the apostle Paul put it, a time is coming when we shall meet with God face to face and share his glory, but at the moment 'we see in a mirror dimly'. The vision is clear to the eye of faith, but as far as the reality of physical existence on earth is concerned there are many problems which will now confront you as a Christian. I am convinced that if you stick firmly to this one and only central truth of your salvation in Christ, namely, that the righteous *live* by faith, you will never find any of these problems a stumbling-block to you. On the other hand I am equally convinced that the man of faith does not turn his back on problems, pretending they do not exist, with such pious phrases as 'I'm leaving it all to the Lord'! Instead, because of his faith he makes a genuine attempt to come to grips with his difficulties and to discover how best he might approach them.

Broadly speaking there are two kinds of problems which will cause you trouble, coming to you in varying intensity depending on your circumstances. These are the problems of the mind and intellect, and problems of action and behaviour. To deal with them in detail in this chapter is obviously impossible. My main purpose is to draw your attention to the fact that problems will come and to give you some general guide-lines as to how you might tackle them.

As far as the intellectual problems are concerned, one of the first questions you will almost certainly have to face is, 'How do we know the Bible is true?' Now many Christians (though not all) believe that the Bible *is* the Word of God. That is, from cover to cover they accept it as God's truth for mankind. In that case, since the Bible says that all adulterers shall be stoned, why don't we go to Soho (and other places) and have a field-day stoning all the adulterers? (Most of them are stoned anyway!) Supposing

'I'm leaving it all to the Lord'

I answer my own question by saying, 'Well, of course, Christ gave us a lead about this passage of Scripture when the Pharisees wanted to stone the woman taken in adultery. He said, "I do not condemn you. Go and sin no more." ' Surely am I not then saying that the part of the Old Testament concerning stoning adulterers is out of date and cannot be claimed as God's Word any longer?

This is a problem indeed, and I could spend time answering the query. But in my view there is little point in doing so, for afterwards I could raise a hundred similar difficulties. In any case, there are many good books around which deal with this sort of query in much better detail than I can manage.[1] But I would at this stage like to mention three general points that will be of some immediate assistance to you in sorting out problems relating to the Bible.

First, the Bible is a great mixture of writings and it is consistent with the view that the Bible *is* the Word of God from cover to cover to point out, nonetheless, that it contains a variety of differing literary devices such as poetry, history, songs, parables, symbolic visions and the like. All these writings occurred within a historical context and many of them are evidently straightforward historical records. But while you can obviously take the book of Kings as literal history, you are certainly not intended to take the book of Revelation in the same light. Therefore, as you read the Bible, you must make sure that you are aware of the type of writ-

---

[1] See, for example, R. M. Horn, *The book that speaks for itself* (IVP, 1969); J. W. Wenham, *Christ and the Bible* (Tyndale Press, 1972), and *The goodness of God* (IVP, 1974); A. M. Stibbs (edited by D. and C. Wenham), *Understanding God's Word* (IVP, 1976).

ing in front of you. And, as I say, there are many useful guides for this purpose.

Secondly, the view that the Bible is just a load of myths and fairy-tales is beginning to look a bit shaky these days. Nonetheless, it will be worth your while to read some general books which demonstrate how accurate the historical sections of the Bible are. In this connection the work done by biblical archaeologists can be especially helpful. See, for example, the article by Professor D. J. Wiseman on archaeology in *The New Bible Dictionary*[2] and the same author's *Illustrations from biblical archaeology*, if you can find a copy second-hand. A more recent book and a useful introduction to the whole subject is *The stones and the Scriptures*.[3] Now archaeology does not prove that the Bible is true; but it does provide a wealth of factual support for much of the historical detail recorded in the Bible. But then, even if shown to be historically true, how do we know that what the people said is also true in every respect? People are well known to be liars and the religious world is flooded with a host of books claiming to be the revelation of God. What makes the Bible different from other books having a similar claim?

Well here, and this is my third point, the subject of prophecy comes in. The Old Testament makes some remarkable claims about a number of places in Palestine and elsewhere and many of these prophecies are still being fulfilled today, some

[2] Edited by J. D. Douglas (IVP, 1962).
[3] E. M. Yamauchi, *The stones and the Scriptures* (IVP, 1973). See also A. Rendle Short (revised by Alan Millard), *Archaeology gives evidence* (IVP, 1962).

two to three thousand years after the event. The fulfilment of such prophecies cannot be put down to luck. Rather it suggests that the writer really did get his information from a supernatural source, in a word, God. You will find some useful films produced by a company called 'Fact and Faith Films' which illustrate this point in more detail.

In the final analysis, however, it is your faith which will make the truths of the Bible apparent to you as you read it, though this is not to throw scorn on attempts to give a rational explanation of the events which the Bible records. One note of caution: while the kind of prophecy to which I refer is useful to study, be careful of those who will tell you all about the end of the world and what will happen in the next few years, giving you a detailed order of events. Such people are much on the increase these days, both inside and outside the Christian churches, and to get involved with them will only serve to sidetrack your mind from your main purpose of faith in Jesus Christ.

'But what about the problem of miracles?' I can hear someone saying. 'Surely some of them are a bit far-fetched and others have a perfectly natural explanation anyway?' I think it is important to look at miracles from God's angle rather than from our own human viewpoint. You see, if you do not believe in miracles, never fear, for you are in good company. God does not either – though for a different reason! Do you remember in chapter 3 we were saying that God knows everything, that he is everywhere present and that he has all power at his disposal? If that is so, it follows that for God miracles do not exist, for a miracle is only a miracle to the observer who has not the knowledge or power to explain what has happened. Take the miracle of the crossing of the Red Sea. 'Impossible', said most people a century or so ago. But now we know that there is a natural weather phenomenon which occurs from time to time in that area which still, even in this century, has parted the waters on occasions in the region where the Israelites crossed. The miracle was not so much the parting of the waters as the timing of the event. Mind you, they were not that naïve in Moses' day either. No-one seems to have noticed that, in the account of the miracle in Exodus, Moses records that the Lord sent a strong east wind which parted the waters. It's a pity some educationalists such as Goldman had not read their Bibles more thoroughly before they launched prematurely into such sweeping statements about this and other Bible stories. But then, that's another tale altogether.

All right, so this kind of miracle can be seen from a different angle. 'But what about the resurrection from the dead?' some of you might be saying. Well, here again, the same applies. Certainly neither you nor I can raise anyone from the dead. But since God is all-powerful, it is no problem to him. The resurrection of Christ has been investigated on many occasions and by many people and I would challenge anybody to prove that the accounts relating to it are unhistorical.[4] This is really the miracle of miracles. If it did not take place, Christianity falls to the ground. As Paul again says, 'If Christ has not been raised, your faith is futile and you are still in your sins.' But we have

---

[4] Two of the most useful treatments are Sir Norman Anderson, *The evidence for the resurrection* (IVP, 1950) and Frank Morison, *Who moved the stone?* (Faber, 1930).

no need to fear. Raising people from the dead is to God just like waking people from sleep. At least, that is more or less what Jesus said to Jairus and his wife as they stood gazing at the lifeless corpse of their daughter. Well, the onlookers, of course, did not believe that sort of rubbish. What charlatan was this who gave the parents such false hope by saying their daughter was merely asleep, when to all who were present it was quite obvious she was dead? What Jesus meant, of course, was that raising from the dead for him was like waking up a friend from sleep for us, and he proved what he meant by bringing the little girl back to life again. No. Do not worry too much about miracles. Look at them from God's point of view and you can afford to forget the problem.

A subject which frequently upsets many a new Christian is the question of hell. 'How can a loving God, who did all these things for us, and more besides, which you rave about in your book, condemn people to an eternal life of utter and complete loss?' Well, here again we are bedevilled by terrifying imagery of hell as a place of fork-tailed demons and infernal fires, coupled with a picture of a God of wrath sitting up in heaven delighting to throw his unbelieving creation into an eternity of torment. This is a picture which owes much more to the imagination of writers such as Dante and Milton than it does to Scripture. The Bible view of hell is not like this at all. We have already seen that sin and death are real (not that we needed a great deal of proof here), and you yourself may have already accepted the gift that God offers you, that free gift, you recall, of eternal life in Christ Jesus our Lord. Now this is fine. But think for a moment. There are many who don't want to accept this free gift which God offers. If I offer you a cheque for a thousand pounds, and you refuse it, you are a thousand pounds the poorer as a result. If God in his goodness offers mankind a free gift of eternal life and some refuse it, then it follows logically that they do not receive eternal life with God. Not to receive eternal life with God is described in the Bible as hell – and I can think of no better word by which to describe it. Remember our blind man in the first chapter? If people want to choose to walk over the cliff, we cannot stop them; for the very idea of love and faith implies individual choice. God doesn't force himself upon an unwilling recipient. But make no mistake about it; this is not what God wants. He does not will the death of one single sinner, but wants all men to come to a knowledge of the truth.[5]

There are a number of other intellectual problems which tend to befog the minds of many. Some of these have already been briefly mentioned in previous chapters (for example, the existence of God). While not pretending to have exhausted their number in any complete sense, let us move on to those more personal problems which relate to our actions and, in the process, exercise our intellects as well. If you have not heard it said yet, you soon will, that if you accept Jesus Christ into your life you will have complete victory over sin. This is another one of those dangerous half-truths that can be very upsetting to the new believer in Christ for, in one sense, it is right. Because of our sin, death is within us and

[5] For a detailed study of this problem see J. W. Wenham, *The goodness of God* (IVP, 1974).

separation from God to boot. But Christ, you remember, won the victory over sin and its penalty of death, so that we may go free from that penalty, be forgiven our sin and receive the free gift of everlasting life. This means that, once you trust in Christ and are counted righteous by faith, you have complete victory over the penalty of sin and can say, 'The sting of death is sin, and the power of sin is the law. But thanks be to God, who gives us the victory through our Lord Jesus Christ.'

But most new Christians and, for that matter, many older Christians as well, do not assume that victory over sin means this at all. They think it means that they will have great personal victory in their lives over that sinful nature that rears its ugly head all too frequently and that, in due time, probably sooner rather than later, they will be *completely free* from their sinful nature and its accompanying problems of hate, jealousy, lust and the like. It all sounds so simple; but I am afraid it is not so easy as that. While you are alive on earth you will always have within you the law of sin in your natural body and it will always be at war with the law of God in which you now delight in your inmost self. Many a time, if your Christian faith is genuine, you will say to yourself, 'Wretched man that I am!' And on many occasions you will draw yet again on the righteousness which is counted to you through faith in Christ. So then, along with Paul, with your mind you serve the law of God but with your natural body the law of sin. The victory that Christ gives you now is that he does not condemn you any more for the sinful nature that you have within you. Through his strength you will be able to control and overcome its effect upon your life and in this you can rejoice. But you will never get rid of that sinful nature this side of the grave and it's a good thing really, for, as I said before, it keeps you humble.

But let me emphasize again: this does not mean that we can be unconcerned about the fact that we still think to sin, and still indeed do wrong. Paul says quite clearly that we must not let sin *rule* in our natural bodies and that we must not obey the lusts that we have within ourselves. He says that we should not yield our bodies to sinful actions but yield our bodies to God, so that he can use them as instruments of righteousness. And then he says something which brings great comfort to me when I am forcefully reminded that I am still very much living with my sinful nature. 'Sin', he says, 'will have no dominion over you, since you are not under law but under grace.' In other words, Christ is now ruling in your life through faith, not sin. God's kingdom is set up in your heart; his rule and his dominion is in control, not that of sin, and you are the recipient of the undeserved kindness of Christ himself who, when you fall, is still there ready to pick you up again, dust you down and set you back on the right path.

With this armour at your disposal you will be able to deal with all the personal problems of action which meet you day by day. You will have no need to sweat out nights of 'trysting with the Lord', as some would have you believe, for God is with you wherever you go, and whoever you are with. I could list a whole number of possible problems of action which may come your way, but I think to do so would be superfluous. Nonetheless, a number of pressures will be brought to bear on you concerning the rightness or wrongness of, say, drinking, or what you need to do in order to witness to your faith in Jesus Christ, and so on. I have, in fact, written another book, as yet unpublished, along the lines of some of these problems,[6] and I list below a number of other books which you may find of some help.[7]

Meanwhile, let us return to the theme. In my experience there is nothing particularly spectacular or 'miraculous' about living out the Christian life. God calls most of us to live the life that we have always lived and to do it within our usual surroundings. But he calls us to live it at a new level, which could well mean making some drastic changes in our moral behaviour. There is even the possibility that God might call us to work for him among a remote tribe in Outer Amboina (and I bet you don't know where that is!). But for most of us the normal ways of living out our lives will be pursued. None the less it is important to realize that we shall bring to the task a dimension which will completely revolutionize the ordinary because we have the righteousness of God imputed to us. 'Counted' is the word I have used on previous occasions; but 'imputed' is the more usual word used by Christians. It means 'to attribute' or 'to ascribe'. What is more, we have faith in the ever-present reality of Christ in our lives. We can know his presence with us all the time. Indeed, this latter fact is a miracle of spectacular proportions which is true for the justified Christian and it outstrips all modern-day miracles. I am always baffled by

[6] Derek C. James, *How to be spiritual in eleven easy lessons*.
[7] David Watson, *Live a new life* (IVP, 1975); Michael Griffiths, *Consistent Christianity* (IVP, 1960); James Philip, *Christian maturity* (IVP, 1964); Paul E. Little, *How to give away your faith* (IVP, 1968).

those Christians who speak of Jesus as being 'far from me today' or who come out with such phrases as 'I'm not walking very close to the Lord these days', or 'I wish Jesus was with me all the time'. For whatever our feelings might be, the one who is justified by faith *has* Jesus with him all the time and as close as he possibly could be. Jesus himself said that he will never leave us nor forsake us, and what greater miracle can one wish for than that?

So with the peace of God always with us and his love poured out into our hearts, together with his Holy Spirit, we shall be able with this assurance to tackle any problem that may come our way in the practice of our faith.

8 Happy families!

So he has arrived! God is real and meaningful. He lives in our lives by his Spirit and through our lives by his love. What more can you want? Well quite a lot, in point of fact. To return to our question in chapter one, have you ever been to church? Yes! I can hear what you are saying. 'I thought there was a catch in it somewhere. Who the (whoops) wants to go to church?' Before we start thinking about the church and the people in it, let us look at some other activities of life.

As a youth I was an enthusiastic watcher of football; as a young man I became a regular player and later on a referee. In the last few years, however, I have returned to watching again largely due to the fact that I have moved to within two miles of the Dell. For the benefit of the ignorant this is where Southampton Football Club play. There are other reasons, mind you, such as the onset of the middle ages, a fact of which my ten-year-old never ceases to remind me! Now any team has star players and Southampton is no exception. Yet on at least two occasions I have seen them play clubs in lower leagues and lose. The reason to me has always been obvious, the star players lacked support from the midfield and were consequently starved of the ball. Hence no goals; hence they lost. Football, you see, is essentially a team game. Individual stars have their attraction, but you will never find yourself on the winning side unless you play the game with others.

Now the same applies to the Christian life. Just as football is best learnt and most appreciated by joining a team, so the Christian life is much more satisfying when shared with others of like mind, and when together you are able to worship the God whose abundant grace has been shown to you with such extravagance. I suppose one can get a certain amount of satisfaction by kicking a ball up against a wall, but if this was the only attraction in football it would soon die out. So with the church. Many people say, 'Surely I can worship God by myself?' Well, yes, you can; but an individual needs to share his Christian life and his worship with others of similar mind, otherwise he runs the risk of becoming an island and finding his Christian life becoming less and less attractive, until eventually it flickers out and dies.

Now I could support this point I am making by quoting scriptures in the Bible that exhort us to worship and to meet with other Christians, but I am sure you would be better served by finding them for yourself. If you want some help along this line chapter 5 of David Watson's *Live a new life* and Michael Griffiths' *Cinderella with amnesia* will give you a lead.[1] More to the point is that, while it gives us great cause for being happy to know and experience the grace and mercy of Christ, when we come to share this with other believers and try to work with them it seems to stretch all our powers of love and tolerance. The Christian churches and the

[1] Both books are published by IVP.

Christians in them are often seen to be such poor examples of Christ's love. What is more, if you chance to read a book on church history, it seems to be nothing but a catalogue of arguments, divisions and splits.

Now although this is true in some measure, it is important to remember that, before we trusted Christ, we were looking at the church from the point of view of the outsider, whereas now, being able to recognize more easily our own failings, we shall find ourselves more inclined to accept the failings of others. But in maintaining that it is infinitely more important to join a church than to remain in splendid isolation, it is nonetheless of equal importance to recognize and come to grips with the failings of the church. So, first, let us investigate some criticisms levelled at this militant company both from outside and from within its ranks and see if they measure up to the light of truth.

It is common knowledge today that church membership is falling and that very few people go to church compared with, say, fifty years ago, or even fifteen years ago. Yes, it is common knowledge. But is it correct knowledge? This kind of view has been propounded in good measure by the mass media for the last decade, probably due to the influence of self-confessed humanists and their bedfellows. If we hear this kind of indoctrination frequently enough, after a while we come to believe it. But the real picture is totally different from the impression with which we are usually left. How frequently do we hear the view expressed that the church is patronized by old-age pensioners and children, backed by a score of emotional and eccentric women? Yet the figures of surveys, taken at their most conservative estimates, present an entirely different picture.

Taken in terms of church attendance, 13% of the population are in church every Sunday.[2] I find great difficulty at school convincing prejudiced pupils that this represents a grand total of about 7,150,000 people and that this in turn means that twelve times more people go to church on Sunday than watch professional football on a Saturday afternoon. Now while these figures might represent a decline in comparison with pre-war days, they are still very compelling. And when you realize that the group of protagonists (the British Humanist Association), who have done as much as anyone to spread this false rumour, had a total nationwide membership of 3,083 in 1971 and that since 1967 its membership has declined by 18%, one begins to wonder who is the pot and who is the kettle. In fact, in recent years their membership has declined still further, for in December 1974 it stood at 2,587. So in terms of numbers you will not find the churches empty. My own church and many other churches which I visit from time to time are always comfortably full, and on special occasions, unless you get there early, you will not even get in, let alone get a seat!

Then there is the accusation that the church is full of hypocrites. This one is more difficult to assess and, in any case, impossible to deny. But again, let us look at the accusation more closely before we use it as an excuse not to go to church. If a person worships God on Sunday and fiddles his income tax return on Monday, he is a hypocrite. Now I, of course, would

[2] Peter Cousins, *Why we should keep Religion in our Schools* (Falcon Booklet, 1969).

never dream of fiddling my income tax return! But I wonder how often I have been unnecessarily abrupt – or even rude – to a colleague of mine on Monday after having been to church on Sunday? This is just as much hypocrisy. In other words, which one of us is not a hypocrite at some time or another? Now this is not to excuse hypocrisy. But if you recall our earlier chapters you will remember that the Christian is in no sense claiming moral perfection here on earth. What he would claim is that, because Christ's Spirit is within him, he realizes that he has been rude to a colleague and that this is wrong. Christ then gives him the courage to apologize to his colleague, something which none of us likes to do, particularly if that person is not too endearing or, even more humiliating, a pupil.

A final point on hypocrisy. If you think the church is full of hypocrites, while this is an exaggeration you will find yourself in very good company. As we saw in chapter 4, Jesus was far more scathing in his condemnation of the Pharisees and their hypocrisy than he was of the woman taken in adultery. Yet it was still his custom to worship in the synagogue on the sabbath day. So – I agree; there are hypocrites in the church. But this is no reason for not worshipping God at church, although we must all make certain at the same time that we are not being hypocritical in our own behaviour. If you concentrate on the plank in your own eye, you will be far more tolerant of your neighbour's splinter! This is from the Sermon on the Mount, you know. Recognize it?

There is one other criticism of the church which I would like to tackle – not, I hasten to add, that this in any sense exhausts their number. But I would like to air this one as it rarely meets the light of day, especially amongst Christians themselves. This is because those who feel this fault most are generally least able to express it in Christian circles. I refer to the view that the church is middle-class. Class distinctions still penetrate much of our society, affecting politics, education and much else besides. In Britain the jibe has often been made that the Church of England is the Tory party at prayer while the Grammar and fee-paying schools are their children at study. But to return to the church. Most of its leaders and ministers are drawn from the ranks of the middle-classes and in many cases are totally uninformed and certainly lacking in experience of working-class attitudes and values. A good number come to the job with preconceived ideas that their cultural background is in some way more acceptable to the Almighty than the pop culture of the day, preferring Beethoven to Brubeck, Gounod to Glitter. The fact that a number of these beloved classicists died of venereal disease or had sex lives reminiscent of some modern-day film actresses does not seem to be an inhibiting factor. Incidentally, I am not suggesting that their moral lives should prevent our appreciating their music. It is just that a number of middle-class culturalists often criticize the pop culture of our day for its immoral overtones. They then conclude that it is wrong to participate in, or imitate, the music and style, while at the same time being totally unaware that similar criticisms could be levelled at a number of the classical composers of yesteryear. But I digress.

In these and other ways the impression is given that middle-class culture is, apparently, divinely inspired and infallible. This would not be too bad if we stopped at this point, for a good number of Christians, including the middle-class variety, see this veneer for what it is and have adapted accordingly. But unfortunately these values have spread into our worship and are now almost considered as much a part of the revelation of God as the Bible itself. For example, you suggest to any church that it does away with its authoritarian presentation of the worship service – the 'them and us' situation – and that it should begin instead to involve the congregation in the worship, and you may have a riot on your hands. Some will completely misunderstand you and say, 'Well, we do have laymen reading the Scriptures, you know.' Others will say, 'How can the infant teach its mother?' – a subtle, quasi-spiritual reaction. Yet others will say, 'My goodness, if we do that we'll have them dancing in the aisles, and that would never do, eh what?'

I would like to develop these thoughts at greater length, but this is not the place to do so. I bring this to your notice, however, for one very good reason. You have found a faith in Christ which is real and if you are going to maintain that faith, one of the supports you will need is the companionship, fellowship, love and help of other Christians. This will mean linking up with a church and it is very essential that you do this. You may well find, however, that most if not all the churches in your area have this middle-class, 'establishment' outlook of which I have spoken and initially it may put you off. I would exhort you not to let it do so. Your relationship to Christ is far more important than a load of toffee-nosed culturalists. In any case you will find that most of them, once you apply some of your new-found principles towards them, are not so bad after all. In addition, there is always the possibility that you may be able to introduce some of your friends to the Person you have come to trust. Then, with their help, you can bring your influence to bear, and maybe start altering the system.

Meanwhile, just sit back and occasionally drop the odd bombshell to keep the traditionalists on their toes. You know the sort of thing! 'Why don't we include dancing in our worship? They did in Bible days!' That'll stir them up, you can bet, and at the same time it will test their knowledge of the Bible. You had better check on your own facts first, of course! Then there is, 'Why don't we have armchairs instead of pews?' You will get all kinds of amusing replies to that question. 'We don't come here to sleep you know' (you could have fooled me) and 'What an unnecessary expense!' The last reply will come from the brother who has a colour telly, two cars, and goes abroad for his holiday every year! He will also display a sudden and unexpected urge to help the Third World. Or again, 'Why don't we have a discussion instead of a sermon?' To that the more 'spiritual' ones will start quoting such scriptures as 'How shall they hear without a preacher?' and so on, thus making you look small. But do not give up; you will overcome in the end!

There may be another question looming in your mind at this point, and it is probably something like this: 'Which church shall I join?' The likelihood is that your best solution is to seek the advice of the person or group who introduced you to this book in the first place. But if you are a loner (or even if you

'Why don't we include dancing in our worship?'

are not), in the next chapter I want to look at the set-up of the church in Britain and give you some idea of what to expect. To be forewarned is to be forearmed. In any case, even if you are linked with a church already, you may find the next chapter of value, so read on.

9 All one body we!

The Bible has always taught, and the church has shown remarkable unity in this respect, that, when we speak of the 'church', we do not refer to buildings but to believers. The church, we are told, is the dwelling-place of God on earth; he lives in the hearts and lives of believers; our bodies are the 'temple of the Holy Spirit'. In other passages the Bible describes the believers as 'the body of Christ' on earth. This to me is a rather frightening thought, for Christ, if you like, compresses himself into the lives of those who profess to love him. On the one hand, what a limitation this is for him, yet on the other, what a marvellous privilege it is for us, particularly when you come to look at some of the people in the forefront of church activity.

Most of us are sane and normal individuals but it seems, at times, that the church is full of cranks and eccentrics. I am reminded of the evangelist who would insist on marching through our local streets playing a piano-accordion 'as a witness'. Then there was the vicar who constantly used the phrase 'Praise the Lord' in every other sentence of normal conversation. Mind you, he was very deaf, so perhaps he did not fully appreciate the effect this had on his listeners, particularly the young folk in our church at that time. I remember, too, our camp padre one year – a most saintly man, until he got behind a steering-wheel! Then there was the seasoned preacher who claimed to have 'prayed into' an empty campaign hall the chairs, tables and even the hymn books. For me it conjured up a picture of an animated, Walt Disney-style cartoon!

Yes, there are some peculiar individuals in the Christian church and some would even claim that they are peculiar by design. Yet they all go to make up the church – this body of Christ about which we were speaking earlier. But if at times you find it difficult to appreciate that it is the same Holy Spirit working in the lives of all these differing individuals, then don't be too worried, for you would not be the first to have had that thought cross your mind. But if these folk, and the rest of us who think we are normal, really are the dwelling-place of God himself, why is it, you may ask, that the Christian church has so many divisions within its ranks? I think such a question is now less valid than it was, since, although Christians may still worship in their different buildings, there is frequently today a much greater spirit of co-operation and communion on a variety of different fronts. Nonetheless, in contemplating the problem 'Which church shall I join?' their differences do cause the new believer a bit of a headache. The divisions of the Christian church are far-reaching and have their roots deep in history, often in matters which to the twentieth-century mind seem trivial and insignificant. To give you a detailed history of our denominational foundations would take far too long, even if I could manage to bring a vestige of interest into the exercise. Instead I will summarize the main divisions which are still with us, at least by name, if not by nature.

Saintly, until he got behind a steering-wheel

It is first of all necessary to distinguish between a religion and a denomination. When I joined the Royal Air Force, they asked me to name my religion. 'Christian', I said. 'Oh, you can't have that', they said. 'Why not?' I asked. 'Well, here you're either RC, C of E or OD.' After they had interpreted this nomenclature for me, I said, 'And what if I am an atheist?' 'You can't be an atheist in the forces', they said. 'You've got to have a religion.' I then told the gentleman that what he really meant was 'denomination', but when I saw I was getting nowhere I decided that the conversation had better close, and opted for OD.

You see, when we talk of different religions we mean Christianity, Hinduism, Judaism and so forth. But when we talk of denominations we mean different types of churches within the Christian faith such as Roman Catholic, Church of England, Baptist and Methodist, the latter two, together with many others, coming under the Royal Air Force classification of 'OD' or 'other denominations'. Now, while there are significant differences in worship and teaching between the main denominations, there is usually a generally-accepted core which pervades them all to a greater or lesser extent. This teaching is frequently summarized in the creeds or statements of doctrine to which they subscribe. In all of them, Jesus Christ is preached as Lord and Saviour; the Bible is looked to as an authority, or *the* authority, in matters of faith and conduct, and the church is seen as having a certain discipline and control over its members.

It is important, however, to make a further distinction between these denominations and those who, while often calling themselves Christians, are divided into 'sects'. Some of these folk in one form or another deny that Christ is the Son of God, some reject the Bible as the authority for their teaching (though often claiming that they do not), and establish a form of domination over their members which those who have escaped from it describe as a kind of slavery. In this category of 'sects' I would place Jehovah's Witnesses, Mormons, Christadelphians and many others. It is good for the Christian to know something about them,[1] particularly those which may have a good following locally; but the best preparation in the long run is to know your own faith inside out as revealed in the Scriptures.

Having distinguished the religions from the denominations, and the denominations from the sects, my advice to you is to join one of the recognized denominations. But the question still remains, 'Which one?' Well, I cannot answer that for you and, in any case, even within my own denomination there are churches I would not touch with a barge-pole (by now you will have guessed what an awkward customer I can be!). But broadly speaking here are some personal guide-lines which you may, or may not, find helpful.

There are three main divisions in Christian denominationalism – Roman Catholic, Eastern Orthodox and Protestantism. There are few of the middle variety in Britain and America for, as the name suggests, they are found mainly in the Middle East and in countries such as Greece and Russia. This leaves us with Roman Catholic and Protestant. There are many differences between them, but it is useful to remember that the former tends to emphasize the

[1] See M. C. Burrell and J. Stafford Wright, *Some modern faiths* (IVP, 1973).

authority of the church over the Bible, whereas the latter tends to emphasize the authority of the Bible over the church.

Within Protestant Christianity there is a further division, between the Church of England and the 'Nonconformists'. The Church of England is the officially recognized church in England and is sometimes called the 'Established Church'. In Scotland the Presbyterian Church is the established denomination, whereas in Wales there is no officially recognized church and the same is true for the United States of America. Now when the church became 'established' in England there were those individuals who, like today, refused to conform and hence the 'nonconformist' or 'free' churches were created. As far as forms of worship are concerned the Church of England resembles the Roman Catholic Church in that it has a set form of service which is regularly followed. The nonconformist churches, on the other hand, would claim that they are free to worship as they will. In practice, however, a nonconformist service is sometimes more stereotyped than a set liturgy (though don't tell them I said so, will you?). The main churches in this latter group are Baptist, Methodist, United Reform, Salvation Army, Presbyterian, Open Brethren, Pentecostal, Evangelical Free and some Congregational churches which did not join the United Reformed Church. I must say frankly that I am a Protestant and that I feel the correct emphasis is with those who place the authority of the Bible over the authority of the church. But in saying this I am not denying that there are numerous devout and godly men and women in the Roman Catholic Church.

There is, however, a further distinction which I want to bring to your notice, which is probably of equal importance to that of the denominational differences mentioned above. Until the beginning of the nineteenth century the authority of the Bible was rarely, if ever, called in question by those within the church itself, no matter what their denomination. But since that time this simple basis has not been so clearly distinguishable, due largely to attacks on the accuracy and even the truthfulness of the Bible. Many of these broadsides have come not only from outside the ranks of the church, but also from within, and only those who are prepared to study the matter in some detail will be able to appreciate all the finer points. In any case, while the debate has been a vigorous one, it is my own opinion that the discoveries of archaeology have done much to release the hot air and steam engendered by both sides, resulting in a welcome 'cooling off' period. Briefly the argument is this, that the conviction of the early church and of the Reformers that the Bible *is* the Word of God has been replaced in the minds of some Christian leaders with views ranging from the idea that the Bible only *contains* the Word of God to the position that it is just a human document like any other collection of religious writings, and as such may be followed or rejected at will.

I have already suggested a number of books on this subject which you may well find helpful.[2] My own firm belief is that the Bible does not just contain the Word of God but is, in fact, God's revealed Word to us and, as such, it should be our authority in all the things we do and believe. Indeed this is not

[2] See p. 83.

just my own personal whim, but the historic Christian position down through the ages, so I am not advocating anything particularly revolutionary or 'way out'. Furthermore, I would maintain that the surest way for a new believer in Jesus Christ to grow in his faith is to meet and worship with a church that works from this basis and for him to fashion his life according to the principles of biblical teaching. Again I must stress that there are many devout Christians who would not fully agree with me, but in the words of the apostle Paul I consider this approach to be 'the more excellent way'. These differing attitudes to Scripture cut across the boundaries of denominations so that a Free Church minister may find, for example, that on this subject he has more in common with the Anglican vicar down the road than he has with some of his fellow Free Church pastors. It is also seen in the way in which a common acceptance of Scripture as the Word of God often underlies the work of interdenominational organizations. It is, in fact, surprising how many areas of Christian activity there are where denominational differences are of little consequence.

So, take your pick – or your shovel – and join a church. It is a funny institution, I must agree; but it is not a good thing to give it a miss. You may feel it is rather uncharitable on my part to point out some of its failings, but not to do so would give you a false impression of the institution you are about to join. In any case, it is a fact that there are differing voices within the church and it is my hope that, despite these differences, the all-important principle that 'the righteous shall live by faith' will shine through in your life. Join a church that has this as its main theme and you can't go far wrong, for it was this discovery on my part that inspired this present volume. I had always lived a happy life as a young Christian and had never been dogged by many of the spiritual problems which seemed to hang like a millstone round the necks of several of my fellow Christians. But in my earlier Christian life I could not have given a theological explanation as to why this was the case. Goaded by those who claimed special paths to righteousness and spiritual maturity, I set out on a lengthy period of studying the Bible and the sixteenth-century Reformation almost, as it were, 'by chance'. As a result of these studies I came to understand in my intellect as well as in my experience the truth that the only real basis for a lasting and happy relationship with God is to be found in the words, 'the righteous shall live by faith'.

This fact implies the certain knowledge that we are freed from the penalty of our sins and receive forgiveness through the sacrifice of Christ, and that we do not have to pay back our debt to God for this salvation by doing anything 'religious' in whatever form, though religious activities may have their place in a different context. Because of this justification we are counted righteous by God and as a result we do not need to increase our righteousness by any special experiences, actions or spiritual exercises. Indeed such activities are unable to help us in this respect, because our salvation from the penalty of sin and the righteousness we receive are totally and utterly a free gift from God – we can do nothing to earn them. We just *receive* them through faith. It is *because of this faith* that we have the love of God shed abroad in our hearts together with his Holy Spirit and we are thus able to do all kinds of things which bring credit to Christ's name. But we cannot boast about them because they come from God through our faith.

When you have joined your church, let me offer you one final piece of advice. Do not flit about from church to church. On the other hand, if you do feel that after a reasonable testing period you have joined the wrong fellowship, then do not be afraid to move elsewhere. Only do not make a habit of it, because if you do you will be of no use to God or the church.

God, then, is in this sense restricted by fallible human beings. But he has chosen it this way and I guess he knew what he was doing. For if your church is successful, what have you got to boast about? It is only God working through you to bring about his divine purpose and will on the earth. And if you think your church is not very good and leaves a lot to be desired, then with God's help set about changing it, for that is exactly why God has placed you there. So let us roll now to the final score, for Jesus is coming again, make no mistake.

10 The end is nigh!

As the chapter title suggests, I think the time has almost come for me to lay down my typewriter. There is a lot more I could say, particularly about righteousness through faith – indeed, I could eulogize on this theme for ever. What is more, I have it on good authority that this will probably be one of our main themes in the everlasting kingdom, as well as down here, so perhaps I will still be typing in eternity, that is, if God has got a typewriter. But I think it is about time I left you to start working out your own salvation in your day-to-day living. And you have no need to fear, you know, because God is working in you anyway, carrying out his will in your life.

Before I quit, however, there are three things, 'nay four' (to imitate the old-fashioned version of the Bible) that I want to bring to your notice because of their considerable importance for every Christian, providing you do not make them into a fetish. One of them I have already dealt with at some length; a second I have recommended by implication throughout the book; but of the third and fourth I have made little mention.

The first is to exhort you to join other Christians in a local church if you want to maintain your faith; and I have said enough about this already.

The second is to read the Bible, for this is an important part of Christian growth. If we read the Bible, understand what it says, and then put its principles and precepts into practice in our lives, we shall find that our contact with God, or 'communion with God' as it is sometimes called, will be greatly increased. The first thing to do is to get a modern version which you will find a lot easier to read. Great strides have been made in recent years to bring the language of the Bible up to date with modern word usage so that it is more intelligible to the average reader. I personally like the Revised Standard Version best, backed up with a recent translation called *Good News Bible*: Today's English Version (the New Testament is called *Good News for Modern Man*).

It is regrettable, but unfortunately true, that there are still a number of Christians who persist in perpetuating the Authorized Version of the Bible, either by insisting on its use in church or by writing articles in magazines defending its alleged value and accuracy against the modern versions. Such people seem to be displaying a death-wish on the part of Christianity, being determined that the Authorized Version will persist, even though it is unlikely that it will ever be read and understood by the 'man in the street'. In case you do not realize it, the Authorized Version was translated into English in 1611, so its language is obviously hopelessly out of date. Apart from that, a large number of documents concerning the Old and New Testaments have been found since then, and these have greatly assisted scholars in providing a translation more accurate than was possible 350 years ago.

It's a funny thing, you know, but Luther had the

same problem concerning versions of the Bible at the time of the Reformation. Then the church insisted on covering up God's Word in the language of Latin. Today, as we have seen, some try to cover it up in the language of Shakespeare as if there were something sacred about his words and language in contrast to modern-day words. Shakespeare of all people, who at times used this so-called reverent language to write the most vulgar filth. Still, that's how it goes!

Now that you have got your Bible, the rest is quite simple – read it! When we do so, God puts ideas into our minds and it is as though he speaks to us. That is why it is called 'God's Word', for it is what he has to say (his word) to you and me. But some people treat the Bible like Old Moore's Almanac. They shut their eyes and open the book at any page, expecting God to speak to them from the line they chance to look at. You may have heard the story of a desperate man who did this on one occasion and, opening the page, his eyes lit on the words 'Judas went and hanged himself'. You would not describe this as exactly encouraging, so he had another go. This time he read 'Go and do likewise'! Nothing daunted, he decided to make a third attempt, and on this occasion he saw 'What you plan to do, go and do quickly'. No! This is not the way to use the Bible.

On the other hand some people go to the opposite extreme and make their Bible-reading a drudgery. They find themselves bogged down in a particular routine of time and place which knows no variety, part of it being the need to answer a series of pre-digested questions which may seem to have little relevance to their own lives. Now Bible-reading systems have their place,[1] and I have certainly used some of them myself; but if you are not careful they can easily become a form of legalism for you. That is, you will assume that, because you read your Bible for half an hour each day following system 'X', you are, as a result, doing God a favour and that he ought to be very pleased with you. Certainly we need to read the Bible and we need to read it frequently, not because we are forced to read it but because we want to read it. But avoid getting bogged down in a routine; it can kill your enthusiasm. I am a great believer in change – it is the spice of life; routine kills.

For starters, why not read stories that interest you for one reason or another? David and Bathsheba, for example (you may have seen the film), Saul and the witch, the capture of Jericho, the crucifixion of Christ (seeing 'Jesus Christ Superstar' or 'Godspell' may spark off your interest here), Paul and the riot at Ephesus. Genuine interest will then lead you to study related accounts of the lives of these people and you will no doubt find that the films or musicals you have seen, though whetting your appetite, in fact fall rather short of the real David or the real Jesus. Sometimes I find it valuable to read a complete book at one sitting; at other times I read or meditate on just one verse, one phrase or even one word, over and over again. One of my favourite words is 'grace', as you have no doubt gathered, or 'sheer grace' as the New English Bible translates it. I listen to the pop record 'Amazing Grace' and relate my knowledge

---

[1] See *Studying God's Word*, edited by John B. Job (IVP, 1972). This is a symposium of different methods of Bible study, complete with examples.

of this word to the lines of the song and my personal experience as a Christian, and in the strength of this I go for many days. Well, you try anything you like. But never read the Bible out of a sense of duty; look upon it as an intimate conversation with the one you love.

The third point of which I have made little mention is that of prayer. Now there is a lot of rubbish spoken about prayer in Christian circles and this is not the place to endeavour to expose it. I have written on this point and that of Bible-reading elsewhere.[2] Basically the proposition I want to put over to you is this: prayer for the Christian is like the conversation and communion between a man and his wife. Now I happen to live with my wife – strange these days, I agree, but it is true. Ask anybody who knows me. Now, because I live with my wife I tend to talk to her. Sometimes I have a lot to say because I have had a particularly interesting day at school and I want to share my experiences with her. Likewise she often has a lot to say to me, particularly about the children – their actions and words. Christopher has told his Sunday School teacher that I sometimes drink my coffee out of the saucer, and you can bet your bottom dollar (if you'll pardon the expression) that that was round the church in a flash. At other times we sit in the same room for up to two or three hours and do not say a word to each other; yet I am very conscious of her presence and I am glad that she is there. When I am not literally in her presence, she is still 'there' and has much meaning for me as I go about my daily work.

[2] Derek C. James, *How to be spiritual in eleven easy lessons* (unpublished). Much of the material in this chapter is taken from this book.

Now why is this? Well, the reason is quite simple: I love her and she loves me ('enraptured are the both of we. I love she and she loves I, and will through all eternitie', with apologies to Tom Lehrer). We don't find any difficulty in talking to each other at all and we share everything with each other from the most trivial matters, such as the number of shirts she happens to have washed that day, to the most intimate and personal things about ourselves which we would never pass on to anybody else. We do not have to force ourselves to speak to each other; in fact frequently the reverse is true, for we have such a lot to say that we cannot wait for each other to finish so that we can relate our own experiences.

Mind you, there are occasions when it is not always like this! And the reason for this is quite simple as well. I have offended her, or she has offended me, and there follows one of those deadly periods of tense silence, which is broken only by such words as 'What's the matter with you, then?' 'Nothing.' 'Then why don't you speak?' 'Why don't *you* speak?' Fortunately, however, we keep short accounts with each other. The thing which has come between us is usually very trivial, but it has stopped that intimate communion we have with each other. It is voiced and apologies are given and received, and once again that free interchange of patter is restored.

Communion with Christ is exactly the same and it is called prayer. The basis of our Christian experience is love and, if we are a genuine Christian, we shall find no difficulty at all in talking with him whom we love. It will not be something which we do at set times; it will be something which we do all the time. I don't say to my wife that I will talk

'What's the matter with you, then?'

to her for fifteen minutes each morning and evening with double time at the weekends and maybe three times on Sundays. No! We are continually in communion with each other. And when we are continually in communion with God, then we are really praying. The little details of our daily lives, the thoughts that are constantly in our minds, all this and much more is prayer if we are consciously living in the presence of God. 'Ah yes, but . . .' I can hear someone saying, '*who* lives constantly in the presence of God?' Well, this is an idea which I develop much more fully elsewhere,[3] but the simple answer is – *you* do! The man who is truly justified by faith constantly acknowledges his inadequacy before God and through this acknowledgment of faith he is counted as righteous in God's eyes. God, as a consequence, is always with him. Therefore, provided we continually have this attitude of humility before our Maker, everything we say and do will become prayer.

The late Dean Matthews wrote in November 1969 that our normal thinking and reasoning upon all issues, if done to God's glory, are nearer to the real meaning of prayer than those which are spoken out loud on formal occasions. He maintained that the practice of such meditation led one into real communion with God and fellowship with Christ. The magazine *Crusade* for that same month also had an article on prayer in which the writer said, 'Real prayer is a constant awareness of the presence and fellowship of God.'

The time will inevitably come, of course, when you break that fellowship through, say, a jealous spirit

[3] See p. 117, footnote.

or an unkind word. You will then feel the kind of tension my wife and I experience when we are 'not on speaking terms'. This is quickly resolved if you remember that you are counted righteous by faith, the prerequisite being an acknowledgment of your own state of sin. Quickly and in humility you turn to God in the strength of this truth and all is forgiven through the sacrifice of Christ. Once again you are on speaking terms and real fellowship is restored.

So it is, then, that with God we can talk naturally and normally wherever we are and whatever we are doing. We have no need to follow the 'knees bend, eyes shut' routine in order to pray, or any other routine for that matter (the latest seems to be raising your hands towards heaven). Neither do we always need to be mouthing words at God in order to be praying to him; the consciousness of his ever-present reality is prayer in itself. Some people, including Christians, just cannot understand this. They say, 'This may be all right for you; but I must discipline myself to pray.' Strange, really, but I suppose that, when you love someone, you don't need to explain the communion there is between you; you just experience it. Perhaps these folk have missed out somewhere and God's love is not poured out into their hearts. Maybe they do not understand love at the human level, so cannot understand it at the spiritual level. Who knows? Imagine having to discipline yourself to talk to your wife or husband!

These three things, then, will help you to grow up as a Christian – meeting with other Christians, reading the Bible and keeping in constant contact with God. This is called growth in the Spirit, or spiritual growth. Many Christians, you know, never get beyond the infant stage of spirituality. They make a number of elementary mistakes which could so easily have been avoided had they observed some of the basic principles I have already suggested. Many, going it alone, succeed in falling out of their spiritual cots and sometimes there is someone around to pick them up again and put them back inside the safety of their cradle-walls. But all too frequently this is not the case. You have to start off with the milk, of course, and Peter says this in his first letter. 'Like newborn babes, long for the pure spiritual milk, that by it we may grow up to salvation,' he writes. But don't remain in that position. Paul criticized the church at Corinth because they were still 'babes in Christ'. He wrote: 'I fed you with milk, not solid food; for you were not ready for it; and even yet you are not ready.' The Christians at Corinth were doing all sorts of weird and wonderful things, some of them of a very spectacular nature; but they were not growing up as Christians. Paul could not talk to them as spiritual men. So don't remain a spiritual baby, will you?

But what about the 'Nay four' bit? Well, it is simply this: Jesus is coming again. Did you know that? Well, you do now! And when he comes he is going to raise up from the dead all those who have trusted in him. Then those who are still alive on the earth and are believers will join those whom Christ has resurrected and the great eternal kingdom will commence. When that happens not only will the rule of God be in our lives, but our lives will go on for ever in him. For the first earth will have passed away and there will be a new heaven and a new earth. God will live with us and we shall be his people.

He shall wipe away every tear from our eyes; and death shall be no more, neither shall there be mourning, nor crying, nor pain any more, for all these things will have passed away. But nothing unclean shall enter this heaven; and we know this to be true, don't we? For those who believe are allowed to enter only because Christ has counted them as clean and law-abiding and has forgiven their sins. Then indeed we shall see the light, for in this heaven they shall have no need of sun or moon to shine upon it, for the glory of God is its light, and we shall reign with him for ever and ever. What a prospect!

What amazing grace . . . 'that saved a wretch like me! I once was lost but now am found, was blind but now I see'. This kindness of God, so undeserved on my part, is the basis, the *only* basis, for those who would be truly happy and truly free. With this spiritual experience continually ours, we are not only just, in time – but also for all eternity.

Some Further Reading from IVP
(*Books specially recommended by the author)

TWO USEFUL INTRODUCTIONS TO THE CHRISTIAN FAITH BY JOHN STOTT

Becoming a Christian

Outlines the steps necessary to becoming a Christian. With more than a million copies sold, this booklet has helped very many to a sound Christian faith and commitment.

Being a Christian

A companion booklet to the above, explaining the privileges and responsibilities of the Christian life.

ALSO BY JOHN STOTT:

Basic Christianity

Translated into twenty-six languages, this brilliant book outlines the main Christian beliefs.

*Go free!**
Robert Horn

A clear introduction to justification.

It shows how God acquits us of our sin, and brings us into a dynamic relationship with himself.

Jesus spells freedom
Michael Green

We crave real freedom. In this book the author shows that Jesus was the one really free man, and how we may attain liberation through him.

Take my life
Michael Griffiths

A plea for a whole-hearted Christianity, which takes the Bible seriously and waits to transform our daily living.

*How to give away your faith**
Paul E. Little

A cartoon-illustrated book explaining the art of leading people to Christ. A best-seller on both sides of the Atlantic.

*Cinderella with amnesia**
Michael Griffiths

A very practical discussion of the relevance of the church today, and a trenchant appraisal of how we avoid the real priorities.

*The Lord from heaven**
Leon Morris

Jesus is central to Christianity. In this major book the author outlines the life and work of Christ and highlights our needs and his ability to meet them.

Books for Bible Study from IVP

*Understanding God's Word**
Alan M. Stibbs (revised edition by David and Clare Wenham)

A useful guide for beginners, which includes helpful descriptions of the modern versions of the Bible.

*The book that speaks for itself **
Robert Horn

An introduction to some of the problems which meet the reader of the Bible, and an explanation of such subjects as inspiration and infallibility.

Search the Scriptures
Alan M. Stibbs (editor)

A systematic course of Bible study arranged over three years. Available in three separate volumes or in a composite one.

In understanding be men
T. C. Hammond (revised edition by David F. Wright)

A doctrinal handbook showing the main teachings of Christianity, and leading the student on to mature commitment.

*The new Bible dictionary**

Like its companion volume (*The new Bible commentary*) this dictionary is a basic requirement for any Christian's bookshelves, covering subjects from Aaron to Zuzim.

Recent Books from IVP

– BOOKS WORTH READING!

The cost of commitment
John White

'To follow Christ fully means to take steps along the perilous pathway of trust, roped to the safest guide in the universe.'

Don't just stand there . . .
Martin Goldsmith

The well-known speaker shows the biblical view of missionary life and work, and our responsibility to it.

He gave us a valley
Helen Roseveare

A best-selling missionary biography. Having surveyed her life's work in Zaire (Congo) 'warts and all', Dr Roseveare asks, 'Was it all worth while?'

First-century faith
F. F. Bruce

In this revised edition of *The apostolic defence of the gospel*, 'the leading evangelical scholar in Europe' surveys the teaching of the main letters in the New Testament.

Ask now at your local Christian bookshop for a full catalogue or booklist of IVP books or write today to:

Inter-Varsity Press
38 De Montfort Street
Leicester LE1 7GP